English revised and updated edition (e-book and Print on Demand)

© 2014 by Nordbook UG (haftungsbeschränkt), Bremen, Germany

Original title: Schwarzbuch WWF – Dunkle Geschäfte im Zeichen des Panda
© 2012 by Gütersloher Verlagshaus, Gütersloh, Germany
A division of Verlagsgruppe Random House GmbH, München, Germany

All rights reserved. No part of this publication may be reproduced, stored in or introduced into a retrieval system, or transmitted, in any form, or by any means (electronic, mechanical, photocopying, recording or otherwise) without the prior written permission of the publisher.

First Edition

Translation: Ellen Wagner

Designed by: Dirk Osmers, Strombuch.com

Set in Minion Pro and Roboto

ISBN 978-1502366542

For more information please visit our website: www.pandaleaks.org

Bibliographic information published by the Deutsche Nationalbibliothek

The Deutsche Nationalbibliothek lists this publication in the Deutsche Nationalbibliografie; detailed bibliographic data are available on the Internet at http://dnb.dnb.de

WILFRIED HUISMANN

PANDA LEAKS
The Dark Side of the WWF

NORDBOOK

"It's easier to penetrate the CIA than the WWF."
Raymond Bonner, New York Times reporter

"In the event that I am reincarnated, I would like to return as a deadly virus, in order to contribute something to solve overpopulation."
Prince Philip, Duke of Edinburgh, in an interview with the dpa, August 1988

Contents

1. The Bride Wears Panda 11

2. In the Lion's Den 15

3. On Tiger Safari 20

    The Hunters and the Hunted 25
    The Tiger Woman 30
    Ullash Kumar 34
    A Visit with the Honey Gatherers 37
    Land Grab 41

4. Fishy Friends 47

    The Salmon King 50
    Swimming Pharmacies 53
    When Panda Met Salmon 56
    Death in a Cage 60
    Petter's Happy Salmon 65
    In with the Sharks 70
    Pandas Don't Bite 73

5. It All Began in Africa 80

    Grzimek's Mission 81
    Prince Philip Comes Aboard 85
    Gerti the Rhinoceros 88
    Oil in Their Blood 89

Old Pals...92
Skeletons in the Cupboard 98
Operation Lock...104
The Purge of the Batwa...112
The Return of the White Hunters 118

6. Have a Nice Death with the WWF 122

Borneo Ablaze 123
In the Fairytale Forest..128
Greenwashing 134
The WWF as a Business Model......................................137
A Night in Sembuluh...141
The Palm Oil War 145

7. Eco-Indulgences for Sale 150

The Philanthropic Bank...151
An Uprising in Sumatra 153
Certification: We Can Get It for You Wholesale 158
Cultivating Champions 162
The Broken Heart of Borneo...164
We Feed the World...166

8. A Tango with Monsanto................... 170

Membership Number 572...174
The Soy Dictatorship...176
A Patriarch's Dialogue 179
On the Soy Highway..184
Soy Leftists 187

In Monsanto's Close Embrace 189
Pizarro 194

9. Redistributing the World 207

The Pact 209
Jason Clay 212
Blackwater 215
The Friends of Europe 217
Eating Ice Cream for the Rainforest 221
WWF Superpower 232
The Conquest of Papua 239
Kasimirus's Last Stand 245

Acknowledgements 250

Wilfried Huismann 251

Endnotes 252

Picture Credits 256

1. The Bride Wears Panda

I ran into Abiud at my local organic farmers' market in Bremen. He was just back from getting married in his native Mexico – in Chiapas of all places, the epicenter of the Zapatista rebellion. Days after his return Abiud still seemed out of sorts. He had discovered that the city of San Cristóbal, far from being seized with revolutionary zeal, was now in the iron grip of the Coca-Cola Company. Upon entering the city's historic baroque cathedral Abiud had been greeted by the deafening rumble of hundreds of worshippers crouched on the bare stone floor, praying fervently to their ancient Mayan gods. Many of them then rose to engage in ecstatic, trance-like dance. Abiud had put this down to the ritual imbibing of pox, the local sacred schnapps. Pox causes belching, a proven traditional method of expelling evil spirits. But when he took a sip Abiud had almost retched: the indigenous tipple had been replaced with Coca-Cola.

It turns out a partnership deal had been done with the global corporation: in exchange for financial contributions to the church all drinks but Coke had been banished from the Temple of God. The beverage sections of local supermarkets likewise now stock only Coca-Cola – shop owners receive a bonus for removing all other drinks from their shelves. The streets are littered with empty Coke cans and visitors note the toothless grins of local children. More Coca-Cola is consumed in Chiapas than anywhere else on earth. Coca-Cola has bought the rights to the freshwater springs in the mountains above the city, and it wouldn't be a big surprise to learn that the multinational had also done a mutually profitable deal with the guerrillas in Chiapas. After all, even the comandantes now drink Coke.

Chiapas is a microcosm of a world in which global corporations rule with soft brutality – a potent cautionary tale about the menace of rampant consumerism. If I had told this story ten years ago no one would have believed it. The back-story is this: to improve its bad reputation as one of the world's largest consumers of water the Coca-Cola marketing department set about *"greening"* the company. The sugar-laden soft drink with the notoriously top secret formula proceeded to morph into a *"green"* product manufactured *"sustainably"* to *"conserve the natural resources of the world."* Did the Coca-Cola ad makers' bright, eco-friendly message convince consumers? Hardly.

Thus the company needed to bed down with a fresh-faced bride who would polish its image by association. In 2007 Coca-Cola and the WWF entered a partnership, declaring they would *"join forces to protect the drinking water of the world"*. Coca-Cola products could now sport the prodigious panda – that cute, cuddly, trust-inspiring little emblem especially beloved of children – adding value to the partnership investment by securing future consumer loyalty. WWF endorsement has set the Coca-Cola Company back 20 million dollars – a bargain, considering that market research rankings place the WWF panda among the world's most trusted brand logos.

For its part, the WWF not only gets big money out of the deal but also wins the favor and recognition of big business. I found a video clip on the WWF website: Muktar

Kent, CEO of Coca-Cola, and Carter Roberts, President of WWF USA, on a polar expedition. We see an Arctic snowscape with sunset and polar bears. The WWF chief affirms: *"The partnership brings together two of the biggest brands in the world ... The best and the brightest don't just want to achieve more market share, they also want to be leaders in solving the biggest problems that face the world ... Coke was a logical choice."* His Coca-Cola counterpart, cloaked in polar fur, adds with emotion: *"We're working closely together in order to ensure that many (people), many generations from now will also be able to enjoy the wonderful polar bears, and our planet."*

The WWF top brass like to feel they're on equal footing with the global corporatocracy jet set. Managers from both Coca-Cola and GMO (genetically modified organism) giant Monsanto are trained at the WWF Academy in Switzerland to become *"One Planet Leaders"*, and Neville Isdell, former Coca-Cola Company CEO, now heads the WWF USA personnel commission. He headhunts prospective WWF top management and presents his picks for appointment – the WWF foregoes stuffy old conventions like voting.

Jason Clay, WWF Senior Vice President for Markets and Food, has announced to the world his plan to conclude contracts with the 100 biggest companies in the energy and food sectors, because these businesses control the world's most significant commodities and: *"When they improve, everyone else in the sector will follow suit."* Jason Clay is utterly convinced the big bad boys will indeed *"improve"*, because the WWF is going to *"embrace"* them. It's that simple. Funny no one's thought of it before.

A conspicuously high number of the WWF's corporate cohorts have distinguished themselves in the areas of environmental pollution and the ruthless exploitation of precious natural resources: British Petroleum, Exxon Mobil, Marine Harvest, Shell, McDonald's, Monsanto, Weyerhaeuser, Alcoa and the world's largest palm oil company, Wilmar. The panda makes them look good. But why does the WWF enter into these liaisons? Is this really the way to make the world a better place, or is the organization just selling its soul for cash? Our investigative journey to the dark heart of the green empire would take us across the globe. At the end of it we would see the panda in a whole new light.

Pandas with money slots

2. In the Lion's Den

The international headquarters of the WWF, or World Wide Fund for Nature, is located in Gland, Switzerland, on the shores of Lake Geneva. The building, a gift of German department store magnet Helmut Horten, is a hulking gray concrete block that looks like an aesthetic declaration of war on its idyllic Swiss village surroundings. It was my inaugural visit to the WWF and my bags were packed with weighty questions.

Inside, the corridors and conference rooms were a hive of activity. A global mix of young people wearing jeans, sneakers, and friendly smiles dominated the scene. These international worker bees made a hip, creative, cosmopolitan impression. *"We're one big team"* announced a beaming Phil Dickie, head of PR, as he met me at reception.

Phil Dickie is Australian. On the long way to his office he confided in conspiratorial tones that he had previously been employed in an Australian government *"secret intelligence unit"*. Dickie called Rob Soutter into our meeting. The tall, white South African is an old WWF warhorse who had for years headed the organization's global campaign for endangered species protection and was currently busy organizing an international *"Tiger Summit"* in St. Petersburg – to be hosted by Vladimir Putin. With a wave of the hand, Rob Soutter dismissed all my critical questions about WWF partnerships with industry: *"Coca-Cola is one of our strategic partnerships. You can't change the world with nay saying. The power lies with the corporations. We can only achieve something by working with them."* Coca-Cola had, after all, committed to reducing the use of drinking water in its bottling plants by 20 percent, and to improve its carbon footprint; and there's nothing wrong with joining forces to save the polar bear, is there? Sounds good, anyway.

Established in 1961, the WWF did not grow out of a grassroots protest movement. Right from the start it catered to a core membership of the global social elite.

Wily PR fox Phil Dickie apparently had a hunch that Rob Soutter would be the right go-to guy for us, and proposed him as an interview partner: the WWF had nothing to hide; everything was perfectly open and transparent – fire away with your questions! Okay: What was the WWF position on genetic engineering? It sits down at the Round Table for Responsible Soy with GMO giant Monsanto, much to the dismay of the other major conservationist groups, for whom Monsanto is the devil incarnate. Phil's expression darkened as he spat out a tight-lipped curse: *"That damned genetic engineering"*. Bull's eye.

He pointed out that most European WWF organizations reject GM (genetic modification) technology. Rob Soutter also looked pained. To keep his mood from souring I quickly changed the subject and asked about WWF's species conservation policies – a subject close to his heart. Soutter's face lit up as he invited me to join him for a sunset safari on horseback through the Kaokoveld game reserve in Namibia, to get a first-hand impression. *"Eye to eye with a lion family – such an incredible feeling."* The dream of the untouched wilderness: Soutter was a prototypical old school WWF romantic, which is not to say that he tried to justify the mistakes of the founder generation.

Until well into the 1980s the wild animal parks of Africa had remained firmly in white hands. As Soutter openly admitted: *"that led many black Africans to believe that the WWF was a sort of extension of colonial rule. But we've learned a lot since then and now collaborate closely with local communities. We give them jobs; they understand that the protection of the animals is in their own best interest. That's how it works."*

This patronizing view of the indigenous people struck a discordant note. It sounded suspiciously reminiscent of that worn-out colonial era credo: we enlightened whites know the score and it's our job to take our backward black brothers by the hand and show them how to treat nature. I had to suppress my outrage at the palpable arrogance of my redheaded interviewee. How is it possible to simply ignore the fact that these peoples had lived in and from the forests and savannas of Africa for centuries without destroying them? The African lions, rhinos, elephants and buffalo weren't under threat until the white imperial masters arrived. It was the wild game hunters from the *"civilized"* world who had committed a veritable massacre on the continent. To secure game stocks for the future the colonial administrations had then begun to create *"whites only"* game and nature reserves throughout the southern nations of Africa.

Black Africans have paid a high price for the private paradises built by the whites on their homeland. The parks and reserves always lay claim to traditional tribal areas; they are never set up where whites have settled. Undeterred, Rob Soutter continued his lecture on the WWF's wondrous conservation projects and the *"integra-*

tion" of the blacks. In my mind's eye I pictured long columns of refugees. In Africa alone, 14 million people have been forcibly relocated to make room for wild animals: they are called *"conservation refugees"*.

By that time my patience was running thin; I'd had enough of the small talk at WWF HQ on glittering Lake Geneva, with its yacht harbors and green wetlands, so I interrupted Rob's flow with a provocative request: *"Could we film at the next Panda Ball?"* Soutter's self-satisfied smile collapsed into a lopsided grin: *"I think not. The guests appreciate discretion."*

The Panda Ball is an annual event often held at Buckingham Palace in London, or some other royal venue. Attendance is restricted to the elite membership of The 1001 Club, a sort of WWF secret society. After Rob had regained his countenance, he simply shrugged off the subject: *"The Club no longer has any significance – we've only kept it going out of respect for the late Prince Bernhard of The Netherlands. It doesn't bring in as much money as some might think, either."* As soon as the words had left his mouth, his eyes seemed to flash annoyance – perhaps he was regretting his statement already.

The 1001 Club was founded in 1971 by then-President of WWF International Prince Bernhard of the Netherlands. The German-born prince recruited powerful businessmen worldwide to join the club, but also a few old comrades, whom he knew from his time in the elite Nazi Reiter-SS equestrian unit, and from his post at the Paris branch of the notorious IG Farben. To this day, the secretive WWF order numbers exactly 1001 "initiates" from across the globe. They generally maintain lifelong membership; when a vacancy arises, a select applicant is appointed to fill it.

Prince Bernhard himself remained member No. 1 until his death, aged 93, in 2004. The identities of the other 1000 have remained secret – until the present day. Only a few names have slipped out over the years: Henry Ford, Baron von Thyssen, billionaire Muslim spiritual leader Prince Aga Khan, Prof. Bernhard Grzimek, US Secretary of Defense Robert McNamara, Fiat boss Agnelli, and various members of European royal families: an alliance of money, bloodlines, and the political elite.

The 1001 Club pays the salaries to maintain the WWF International central secretariat in Gland on Lake Geneva. That allows the international leadership to operate independently of the now 90 national WWF sections. The Panda Ball and other discreet get-togethers also offer a good opportunity for discussing the strategic focus of the world's largest conservation organization. The 1001 Club is no sub rosa WWF command center, to be sure. However it most definitely is an old boys' network with significant influence in the corridors of global corporate and policy-making power.

Rob Soutter wanted to know if I had a list of club members, and seemed relieved to hear that I did not. I knew then that I had to get ahold of that list. It could be the key to the inner sanctum of the WWF, and would also provide insight for the five million WWF members worldwide who still have no idea who really pulls the strings in the organization, and why. Their faith in the beneficent panda is, for the most part, unwavering.

3. On Tiger Safari

In the weeks following our initial visit to Gland I received the occasional email from Rob Soutter: everything's fine, look forward to seeing you again soon in Namibia, on horseback. He was too busy just now, however, as WWF's Year of the Tiger was just nearing its climax. As WWF *"Tiger Ambassador"* Leonardo DiCaprio would attend the Tiger Summit in St. Petersburg, where leaders of the seven countries still home to wild tigers would all be on hand, doing their bit to save the last 4,000 of the animals from extinction. Vladimir Putin was hosting the event – he said the tiger was his favorite animal. The Russian leader saw in the Hollywood star an equal, a real *"tough guy"*.

The Year of the Tiger was a chance for the WWF to really strut its stuff: mobilizing heads of state and steamrolling the whole world with a *"Save the Tiger Now"* ad campaign featuring Leonardo DiCaprio. An article appeared in the Washington Post on November 7, 2010 with the byline: Leonardo DiCaprio and Carter S. Roberts. It's headline pronounced: *"If we save the tigers, we'll save the planet"*. An all or nothing proposition. Who wouldn't want to be on board?

After two months of waiting in vain for a binding offer from Rob Soutter I developed a sinking suspicion that nothing would ever come of our horseback ride to the lions. So I decided to set out on my own steam on a journalistic journey to investigate the WWF – and what better place to start than in the tiger terrain of India?

From Raipur we headed north to one of India's oldest tiger reserves, driving through a fertile green breadbasket dotted with idyllic villages. It was a blessing, after the hell-on-earth of Raipur: the dizzying stench of open sewers running alongside the streets; the garbage piled high on the sidewalks, in which boney cows forage for scraps; the deafening noise of aggressive motorcycle traffic, as the drivers threaten to run each other and pedestrians off the road.

A girl of no more than 13 with an infant in her arms slept at the curb, only centimeters from the road traffic, almost invisible beneath the choking black exhaust clouds from the battered old diesel vehicles that filled the streets. The daily fight for survival renders the people both apathetic and ruthless. India's cities are being smothered in filth and garbage. In the year 2050 there will be more Indians than Chinese. Land is at a premium – and the long arm of industrial greed extends deep into India's national parks.

After a six-hour drive on dusty roads we saw the first roadside billboards with the WWF panda logo, urging us to *"Save the Tiger"*. We had reached the buffer zone of Kanha National Park. Many of the current inhabitants of local villages had lived in the forest – before the government resettled them. Apparently, it was impossible for tigers and humans to *"coexist"*. WWF plans for new tiger reserves have led to similar operations throughout India: the mandatory resettlement of forest-dwelling Adivasi tribes – sometimes with the use of military force.

A few kilometers after passing the main entrance an iron gate opened and we drove into the garden paradise that surrounds the Singinawa Jungle Lodge. Lemurs hopped from tree to tree and onto the roof of the bungalow to observe our arrival. Three *"boys"* in post-colonial faux-military khaki uniforms welcomed us, and proceeded to serve a luxurious *"full English"* breakfast. There were only eight other tourists at the lodge, wealthy pensioners from the USA and UK. We quickly developed a friendly rapport with them. They had booked their tour, via a WWF website, with Natural Habitat Adventures, a travel agency that prides itself on being the *"premier travel partner of the WWF"*. The two-week package was called Wild India and had cost 10,000 dollars per person, double occupancy. According to friendly lodge owner Nanda SJB

WWF tiger campaign: "Born to become extinct"

Rana the hefty price tag included the guarantee that every *"adventurer"* would get to see at least one tiger in the wild.

The next morning at five AM we set off. It was only 3 degrees Celsius in the open jeeps, and by the time our convoy reached the main entrance to the park about an hour later some of us already had blue fingers. We joined a long line of waiting vehicles. 155 safari jeeps are permitted entry here each day – not just to the periphery but to the core zone of the park as well, home to most of the tigers. The thrill of the chase was palpable; as soon as the barrier was raised the revving jeep fleet sped forward. I was surprised to learn of the extensive network of broad, sandy paths throughout the national park. Sullen men with brooms are posted roadside, keeping the "tiger highway" tidy for tourists. The sweepers are Adivasi: native forest dwellers. The once proud lords of the jungle have been reduced to acting as menial service providers for the eco-tourism industry.

According to official statistics there were about 100 tigers left in the park at the time of our visit, but our ranger considered this to be sheer propaganda. He put the number at 50 at most – our first lesson in Indian tiger arithmetic.

On our safari we saw monkeys, exquisite birds and a few gaur, or Indian bison – massive gray wild oxen weighing tons, the world's largest living bovines. Every time our ranger spotted an animal he slammed on the brakes. A few seconds' stop for a photo op and then the hunt resumed. But the eco-safari tourists didn't care about bison and monkeys; they had paid to see tigers. The ranger showed us how a tiger marks his territory on a tree: three meters up the trunk the big cat had clawed deep grooves into the hard wood, giving a vivid impression of the mighty animal's strength. In the wild, every mature male tiger claims a territory of 40 square kilometers for himself. At the next crossroads we met up with a mounted tiger-scouting unit: park rangers on elephants. They'd been on patrol for hours, equipped with walkie-talkies, but still no sign of a tiger. If I were a tiger confronted with that hellish noise I too would have taken refuge in the underbrush.

After three hours of cruising the forest, about 30 minutes of which had been spent sitting in traffic jams along the narrow tiger highway, we all met up again at the breakfast grounds. The rangers unloaded food hampers and placed the contents on the linen tablecloths spread over the front hoods of the jeeps: toast, ham and boiled eggs, tea and coffee. The various jeep teams compared notes in hunting jargon – one woman swore she had seen the tail of a tiger on the run.

The grasslands that now belong to the animal reserve used to be home to the Adivasi. Their villages and their culture have disappeared. The tourists don't question this – perhaps the government resettlement scheme appears justified. The WWF would seem to support this view: without explicitly endorsing forced resettlement, for years the organization has propagated the official line: For centuries we human beings have robbed wild animals of their habitat; now it's their turn.

Suddenly a ranger shouted: *"A tiger has been spotted not far from here."* Everyone ran back to the jeeps. The engines fired up and off we went again. We stopped where the tiger had reportedly been sighted. A monkey called out the tiger alarm. Deer raced off through the bush. We observed them being pursued – by a wild boar. Damn, still no tiger! After a short break to grab lunch at our jungle lodge we were back to the tiger terrain. It was a race against time; the park closed at 6PM. After the days outing we'd had enough of the tiger chase, so we spent the second day by the hotel pool. The other safari tourists looked askance at us wimps, but the lady of the house, Latika Nath Rana, acknowledged our decision with a look of gratitude.

The Hunters and the Hunted

Dr. Latika Nath Rana is a tiger researcher with a PhD from Oxford. As the first woman in this specialist field she has achieved a prominent position among her Indian colleagues. At breakfast she confided in me that she's lost patience with her scientific brethren *"We actually already know all there is to know about tigers. They should really just be left alone."* She wasn't best pleased with the WWF tiger campaign, either: *"It's just bringing more and more tiger experts into the country who then lay siege to the animals."* They set camera traps everywhere and shoot the tigers with tranquilizer dart guns so they can hang GPS tracking devices around their necks. The WWF aims to use the data thus gathered – on movement patterns and total numbers of animals in existence – to allocate further tiger protection areas. Dr. Rana was not convinced: *"It's all superfluous; it has no benefit for research. There is only one purpose behind it: the money must be spent."* I asked her about the WWF billboards lining the route to the National Park. She laughed: *"They're good at public relations. But I've yet to see even one genuinely useful WWF project here."*

After careful scrutiny of the WWF India budget Dr. Latika Nath Rana has come to the conclusion that a large part of the WWF donation money from abroad is not spent on specific local conservation projects: *"Most of the funds the WWF gives to official government bodies end up disappearing into the pockets of functionaries."* Registering my baffled expression she added: *"That's nothing out of the ordinary for India. If the donations were to actually make it to the tiger reserves we'd be able to hire four keepers for every tiger, build a protection wall around all 39 of India's tiger reserves, and buy a life insurance policy for every single tiger on top of that."* She said she had distanced herself from all the tiger hype and now focuses her energies on working with the villagers in the buffer zone. *"If we can win them over to our side we'll be able to help the tiger."*

According to Dr. Latika Nath Rana the *"tiger mafia"* had repeatedly found villagers on the peripheries of the reserves willing to act as contract killers for a tiger hit. The hired hunters were paid only a few Rupees for their trouble – they had no idea how much wild tiger products were worth on the global market. In New York's Chinatown the price of tiger bonemeal tea – sold as a powerful male potency potion – now tops that of heroin.

That night at the long dinner table Dr. Rana's husband Nanda explained the origins of the belief widely held in Asia that tiger extracts boost virility: *"It's quite something when tigers mate; they go at it for days on end. One pair of tigers holds the world record: they had sex 113 times in a single day."* Jack from Arizona, who regularly travels to Shanghai on business, argued that there are now well-established commercial tiger breeding farms in China. Our host shook his head: *"That's not much help to us. The Chinese believe that the products from wild tigers have a much better effect."*

Maggie, sitting next to me, had remained quiet during the whole tiger sex discussion, silently basking in the joy of the day's experience: on the afternoon safari her jeep had met up with a real live tiger. She couldn't recall the details because the tiger could only be seen from afar – to her dismay the other jeeps had simply jumped their place in line to get a better look. Nonetheless, Maggie now felt that the 10,000 dollars for her Wild India tour had been well spent. *"Because"*, she announced in a deep tone of conviction, *"we might be the last generation able to see a tiger in the wild. Our grandchildren probably won't have the chance."* The apocalyptical slant of the WWF campaign had obviously found a congenial medium in Maggie. But what did any of it have to do with protecting nature?

After dinner our host Nanda Rana led us into his library to show us a prized possession: large black and white photo prints from the heyday of the tiger hunt. *"These pictures were a gift to my family from the House of Windsor."* I then learned that Mr. Rana is a scion of the Nepalese royal family, who had organized the tiger hunts for the British colonial rulers on their visits "back in the day". He showed us a photo of a group of elephants standing in circular formation. *"Before King George arrived 1000 elephants were rounded up from across the country. They* were used to drive the tigers together and encircle them in a pocket. *On this hunt here they bagged 120 tigers – in one day. Quite an unsporting sport."* The next photo showed dozens of tiger pelts hung up to dry like hand towels on a clothesline.

When I asked whether Prince Philip, Duke of Edinburgh and founding father of the WWF, had been an active participant in these tiger hunts, the Nepalese aristocrat looked at me with a hint of suspicion and decided to take a diplomatic tack: *"He did come along sometimes, but as far as I know he didn't shoot. He was a conservationist, after all. He excused himself by saying he had sprained his trigger finger."*

Contemporary press reports tell a different story: On a state visit to India in January 1961 Queen Elizabeth II and her prince consort went to Rathambore to go tiger hunting. In anticipation of their visit helpers had bound dozens of live goats to trees as bait for the big cats, which the beaters then drove directly into the monarch's firing line. But as soon as the Queen had a tiger in her sights she put her rifle aside and reached for her camera instead, leaving the kill shot to Prince Philip. Soon afterwards the photo of the hunting party was circulating in Great Britain: in the foreground the dead animal lies stretched out, behind it the hosts of the hunting party and the royal couple.

Almost exactly 50 years after this hunting jaunt we managed to secure an interview with Prince Philip at Buckingham Palace. He took our question about the tiger hunt like a man, looked straight into the camera, and confessed his crime: *"I've never been big game hunting. No, never – except that one occasion in India. I've shot one*

Prince Philip during our interview, 2011

tiger in my life, that's all. The only way you can ensure that you get a reasonable wildlife population is by making sure that they're balanced. You can't just leave it to nature because we're interfering with nature all the time. And so you protect some things by doing away with the predators, otherwise it won't work."

It had been a bothersome business nonetheless. The picture of the dead tiger had triggered a wave of indignation in Britain. Such rotten timing! In the spring of 1961 Prince Philip and his pals were just preparing to proudly announce the birth of the WWF to the world. For Prince Philip the group portrait with tiger carcass was purely an image problem. In his view the hunt goes hand-in-hand with animal protection: the only really good conservationists are hunters, as his philosophy would have it. Most of the national parks in Africa and Asia started as private game reserves for the white European and US elite. In 1900 there were still 40,000 tigers in India – before the trigger-happy Windsors and their upper crust crowd arrived to make their contribution to *"conservation"*. By the end of colonial rule the Indian tiger population had been reduced to just 5,000.

Prince Philip with prey and Elizabeth II, 1961

The Tiger Woman

It was late at night and nocturnal wild animals were out on a raid. Vasudha Chakravarthi led the way. Her house was only a few hundred meters away but I was still spooked by the polyphonic murmurings of the forest. She laughed at me and stomped on ahead, armed with a big stick, ponytail swinging jauntily in the moonlight. The young woman had lived in the jungle for the past four years and was not afraid of the wild animals. *"They know me, and know that I'm their friend."* But they didn't know me! We had almost reached her house when she suddenly stopped and stood stock-still, shining her flashlight into the bushes: *"A leopard, very close by."* I asked if leopards are man-eaters. *"No, humans are not part of their diet. They only kill people for the sake of killing."* How reassuring. Vasudha shooed the leopard away with hissing sounds and soon we were finally in the safety of her home, a cabin built 160 years earlier by an Irish couple that had fallen in love with the remote region. An old tin sign still hung above the front door: Hunting Lodge. Vasudha had renovated the house on the edge of the Mudumalai Tiger Reserve in the south of India with her own hands.

Before choosing a life in the wilderness Vasudha had worked in a well-paid job at HSBC Bank in London: *"It was interesting, but at some point I realized that life as a businesswoman didn't make me happy; it was alienating me from myself."* Vasudha's husband didn't share her passion for the wilderness, and they eventually split up.

Every morning Vasudha puts on her camouflage fatigues and heads off with her camera on a tiger-tracking mission – alone and unarmed. She said she had only met up with a tiger on her rounds a total of seven times, and she had never been afraid: *"Once I came upon a tigress that had just killed a deer. I sat just a few meters away from her and began to take pictures. She looked at me and left me in peace. For 40 minutes we sat facing each other. She could have killed me at any time, but I knew she wouldn't. There was a silent accord between us."* Vasudha showed me her tiger photos on her laptop. None of the pictures have been published: *"I couldn't do that to the tigers; it would only bring even more people from the rich countries here to see them."*

We were awakened the next morning by rays of sunlight shining through the cracks of the wooden shutters. Neighbor Antony was already there, just checking to see that everything was okay. He lives three kilometers away, and he'd brought his 10-year-old daughter Preethi along with him. Antony got to work repairing the water pipe that runs from Vasudha's well to the kitchen. An elephant had paid a nighttime visit and trampled on the line.

Vasudha introduced me to her little friend Preethi *"one of the best trackers there is"*. Preethi often joins her on patrol to help find the trail of the tiger – the youngster knows her way around the forest because every day she makes her way on foot through seven kilometers of tiger terrain to get to school. She had recently met up with a tiger with *"a huge head THIS big"*. She recounted the incident with obvious pride, stretching her arms out as wide as she could. Had she been afraid? Preethi looked at me in amazement: *"No, what of?"* She had only ever had one tussle with an animal: on her way home from school an enormous cobra had once attacked her. *"I had to beat it to death with a stick."*

Then Vasudha and Preethi had an idea: the next day we would go tiger tracking together. Preethi had seen a Sambar deer carcass a few kilometers away – the obvious remains of a tiger takeaway – the tiger would likely still be in the vicinity of its prey, because the meal was enough for two or three days. The offer was tempting, but I had

Preethi and Vasudha in the tiger forest

to admit that I was scared. The two of them swore on the tiger god that nothing would happen to me because tigers don't like human blood. But, I argued, man-eating tigers do exist! *"Yes,"* said Vasudha, *"but the man-eating ones are very rare. Normally, tigers will only kill people when they feel threatened, or when they're too old and weak to hunt other prey."*

I politely declined the kind offer – the prospect of being lunch for a geriatric tiger was just a bit too unnerving. But I had disappointed the fearless tiger duo: just another wimp after all, not much better than the self-styled *"tiger experts"* from across the globe that turned up there in droves: *"They should just stay at home."* Because of their fear of tigers they would only enter the jungle in secure vehicles under the protection of armed rangers, disrupting the life of the animals. Vasudha's rage erupted at me: *"Why don't you all leave the forests to the people who live in them? You have the money and the power to penetrate the core zones of the reserves with jeeps. Many wild animals have been killed in accidents with tourist jeeps. And can you imagine the noise pollution that eco-tourism brings? For a few extra dollars the rangers will drive the jeeps right up close to the animals to get them to charge the jeeps – for a special kick. Our elephants used to be the most peaceful creatures imaginable. Now they're so high-strung that attacks on people are becoming more and more frequent. Only yesterday an elephant killed two people in our neighboring village. That's all a result of the Western tiger craze. We don't need your money. Just leave the tigers in peace, maybe then they'll still have a chance."*

Ullash Kumar

Towards the close of the colonial era the British in India and Nepal established the first game reserves there. After their departure the WWF took the reins of the tiger protection efforts and, in 1972, started the campaign "*Operation Tiger*". The organization persuaded the Indian government under Indira Gandhi to create reserves where tigers could live undisturbed by human beings. Local authorities forcibly expelled forest-dwelling tribes; nearly a million people thus lost their home. Yet the tiger population still continued to shrink. According to official data there are now only about 1,700 tigers left in India. So what happened? A lifelong conservationist, a man who had since childhood been intent on helping the threatened tigers, elephants and rhinoceros of his country, had asked himself the same question.

Ullash Kumar lives in the megalopolis Bengaluru, capital of the southern Indian state of Karnataka. The gentle man with soft facial features is a self-described *"wildlifer"* and *"eco-activist"*. I found him via the Internet. I was immediately struck by the clarity and precision of his online articles; it was obvious that the author was no armchair ecologist, but someone who really knows his way around the jungle. I had contacted him via email. Now that we were sitting face-to-face the first thing Ullash revealed, contrary to my expectations, was his deep love of the WWF.

As a schoolboy Ullash Kumar had been a member of the WWF youth club and had gone on excursions into the forest of his homeland, Nilgiri. There the budding conservationists learned to identify animals and plants: *"I'm very grateful to the WWF for that education. After university I became secretary of the Nilgiri Wildlife Association, which works strictly in line with the WWF. We*

Ullash Kumar

fought for the expansion of a tiger reserve. An Adivasi tribe lived in the territory and the plan was to resettle them. It was clear in my mind that they had to go, and I seriously believed they would be happy about it: their pets would be safe from wild animals, they would be able to send their children to school, and to find better jobs than gathering fruit in the forest or tapping rubber trees.

Much to my surprise the tribe fought for their right to stay in the forest, even taking their case to court. I wanted to understand what these people thought and felt, so I decided to go visit them. That was the start of a major transformation within myself, to the extent that I now vehemently reject the Western conservation model. But the WWF continues to pursue its elite conservationist course. It still has no understanding of indigenous peoples."

Ullash Kumar belongs to a network of Indian conservationists who have formed an alliance with the indigenous forest dwellers. *"Only the native tribes can save the tiger and other endangered animals – they are our only hope."* Most Indian intellectuals have no contact with the Adivasi, who are ranked as *"untouchables"*, the lowest rung of the traditional Indian caste system. Like the proverbial leopard that can't change its spots, it seems even dedicated activists have trouble breaking free of the old system.

In the name of the doctrine of the human-free jungle, now, once again, another up to one million Adivasi have been earmarked for resettlement, to make way for the expansion of old reserves and the creation of new ones. Many tribes are now resisting this latest wave of expulsions. Ullash Kumar does not think the compensation money offered will tempt them to part with their forest:

"A tribe gets about 10 lakh rupees compensation for giving up its forest; that's about 80,000 dollars. That's quickly used up. Where are they supposed to live? And what from? No one wants them. They're lost in the big city slums."

On our drive to Nagarhole National Park Ullash explained that Adivasi is a Sanskrit word that literally means *"beginning dweller"*, in other words, the first to live in a place. And the forest-dwelling tribes of India were in fact there long before today's dominant ethnic groups. For decades, the majority population ran roughshod over the rights of the Adivasi. No wonder that some tribes sympathize with the Maoist guerrillas engaged in an ongoing insurgency in India. We stopped in the city of Mysore and bought an Indian Times with the headline: *"Six WWF employees kidnapped"*. Ethnic Bodo rebels had captured the WWF workers as they were taking a tiger census in the jungle of Assam. The army had sent a special unit into the jungle to free the hostages – a day in the life of India. In the area we were heading to Naxalite Maoists had made repeated attacks on police stations and forestry authority offices.

A Visit with the Honey Gatherers

After six hours on the road we arrived at Nagarhole National Park. Monkeys hopped gracefully across the road; now and again we met up with an elephant; and in the dim dusk light the glowing eyes of a leopard beamed at us from the underbrush. The huts of the honey gatherer tribe came into view. A big sign at the roadside just before the entrance to their village read: *"stopping prohibited"*. But we had a special visitors' permit from the park administration. Half the village had come out to meet us. Leading the welcoming committee was tribal matriarch Muthamma, a dark beauty in a long white sari. She got right to the point: *"Ten years ago we were resettled for the first time – and put here, in the buffer zone of the National Park. Now they're expanding the tiger protection area and we're supposed to move again. The government treats us like objects. But we won't budge – the only way they'll get us out of our forest is dead."*

At the time of our visit, 30 villages in the area had been earmarked for removal – a total of 15,000 people. Muthamma maintained contact with the other villages and organized the resistance: *"We've lived together with tigers for centuries; we don't kill them and the tigers don't kill us. We revere the tiger as a deity; we have a tiger altar over in the forest. The conservationists from the city don't understand the forest. As long as we're alive the tigers will still be safe. If we disappear, the loggers and poachers will have free rein."*

According to Muthamma, wild animals had not benefitted from the first tribal resettlement out of Nagarhole National Park; the profits were all on the side of the big-city businesspeople. Only a few years after the government expelled the indigenous people from the forest, certain areas within the park had been converted to commercial forest by the state authorities. In Nagarhole National Park alone, eucalyptus and teakwood plantations now occupy land that was once home to 40 Adivasi villages. Throughout India lumber and construction companies and factories

Muthamma, the tribe's leader

are encroaching on the national parks, decimating them. Often the expropriation of the Adivasi is only the first step in paving the way for the industrial takeover of the forest.

That hasn't stopped WWF India from putting continued pressure on Adivasi throughout the country, at least indirectly. The organization had become dissatisfied with the Indian government because it had let resettlement policy slide in the 1980s – out of indifference, or perhaps also to avoid further conflicts. In August 1997 WWF India ended up obtaining a high court decision that forced the state governments to implement the agreed Adivasi resettlements within a year.[1] The WWF saw in this decision an historic victory for the conservation movement. But it put fear in the hearts of millions of forest dwellers: they would have to pack up and leave their ancestral home. Those who were allowed to stay would have to abandon their traditional economical activities: hunting, fishing and gathering wild fruit.

39

In the view of Indian environmentalist and Greenpeace president Ashish Kothari, the legal decision effected by the WWF was *"suicidal"*: in the wake of the ruling, riots and resistance activities broke out across the country. According to Kothari, *"conservationists who believe that wildlife can be protected in such circumstances are living in a fool's paradise."*[2] From then on the Adivasi saw the conservationists as their natural enemies. The human rights organization Ekta Parishad organized a march of 30,000 Adivasi on the capital New Delhi. There were also isolated acts of violent resistance: out of desperation some tribes had taken the extreme measure of poisoning tigers. No tigers, no expulsion – it was their last hope. The resettlement policy led to violence and chaos throughout the country.

Adivasi resistance to the expropriation was so strong that finally, in December 2006, the Indian parliament passed the Forest Rights Act, for the first time anchoring indigenous land rights in law. According to the legislation each Adivasi is entitled to 2.5 hectares of forestland. Resettlement is permitted only on a voluntary basis. The law sparked vehement protest and legal counterattacks from conservation groups and the forestry authority. In the daily grind of forest management the ruling has often simply been ignored. Illegal expulsions still occur. But at least the Adivasi and other forest dwellers now have a legal basis for pursuing their rights in court. The United Nations also lent its support: in September 2007, the UN General Assembly in New York passed a resolution called the *"Declaration on the Rights of Indigenous Peoples"*.

The WWF is also pleased to point to its own *"Declaration of Principles"*, which states that conservationists and indigenous peoples should become its *"natural allies"* in the *"fight for a healthy, natural world"*. The WWF document clearly recognizes that indigenous peoples *"have often been stewards and protectors of nature"*. Despite this noble declaration, WWF India continues to adhere to its resettlement policy – albeit on *"a volunteer basis"*, as the law stipulates.

Muthamma could only laugh at that. To encourage the willingness of her tribe to *"volunteer"* for resettlement, the forestry authority had prohibited them from exploiting the forestland they had been allotted as compensation in the 1990s. *"We're no longer allowed to keep livestock or harvest honey, the basis of our existence."* According to the forestry authority – mouthing the WWF ideology – their commercial activities spoiled the *"virgin"* status of the forest. How were Muthamma's people managing to survive? *"Every day we're picked up by a truck and brought to a coffee plantation. We have to work there for 120 rupees, (2.75 dollars) a day – half of what the other workers earn. We have to do it; otherwise we'd starve to death. It's their way of trying to demoralize us."*

Land Grab

The prohibition of forest exploitation has led to the creeping loss of Adivasi common property – and ultimately to the demise of their culture; the restriction has sent an army of cheap laborers into the open arms of the plantation economy, which is claiming ever more of the forest. In practice, *"voluntary"* resettlement is nothing more than a soft-sell version of the old government expulsion policy. The *"WWF Declaration of Principles"* makes a good impression at conferences, symposiums and on websites. But it is nothing more than a paper tiger; reality bares its dangerously sharp teeth on the ground, in tiger territory.

Back in the village of the honey gatherers: in the meantime, almost all the inhabitants had joined the circle around us. I noticed that the women were very forthright, contributing freely and with total self-confidence to the debate. I also saw several men in the crowd holding babies; the conventional division of labor between the sexes obviously did not apply. 2,500 years ago, when the Buddha had encountered Adivasi culture on travels across India, he too had been deeply touched by their egalitarian ways. The Adivasi tribes had served as a model for his ideal of a self-sufficient, humanist and democratic society. This was how man should live on earth: without money and without the lust for material possessions. Many elements of this ancient culture are still intact today, but the Adivasi are not immune to the temptations of consumerism. This was illustrated when the hush of the forest was suddenly shattered by the ring-ring of a mobile phone. Muthamma laughed sheepishly as she fished a cell phone out of the folds of her sari. Everyone laughed.

An old man spoke up, introducing himself as Bhaskaran. He had worked as a tracker for the Indian tiger researcher Dr. K. Ullas Karanth: *"We know where the tigers are and can read their pugmarks and the traces they leave behind. He wanted to put collars with electronic tracking devices on the tigers to monitor their movements. To do this, the tigers first have to be subdued with the dart from a tranquilizer gun. For fear of the tiger, the scientists often give them too high a dose, and the tiger dies of cardiac arrest. I've seen it with my own eyes. 15 of the tigers died this way, but they were counted in the tiger census anyway. They just left the transmitters lying in the forest where they keep sending their signals as if the tigers were still alive."*

It is not known whether the WWF is aware of the deaths caused by the tiger researchers. Certainly not a word of it has yet reached the donating public in the West. The WWF continues to solicit for funds for camera traps and the costly tracking devices, although their scientific value is questionable. In a fundraising campaign with the headline *"Tigers in Trouble"* the WWF appealed for a donation of 80 dollars: *"so that we can install camera traps. The images show us where the tigers live. This information is very important and lays the foundation for the allocation and establishment of new protection areas."*[3]

"Unnecessary" said Ullash Kumar, *"if there are tigers living in the forest anyone in the local villages will be able to tell you so."* Tigers leave unmistakable signs to mark their territory. For that reason Ullash Kumar knew the tiger campaign to be useless, but saw it as a big business in India, with many stakeholders: civil servants, tiger experts and politicians. The more tigers an Indian state registers with the central government, the more money it draws from the national tiger budget, which in turn receives international funding.

Tiger conservation policy thus indirectly feeds an enormous and corrupt forest administration. Ullash Kumar told me about the KMTR reserve in Tamil Nadu that had just been declared an *"endangered tiger habitat"*: *"Al-*

though there is not a single tiger left in the area. The last one was seen there 40 years ago by local forest dwellers." According to Ullash Kumar, nature conservation was being used as *"a pretext to get at money and land"*. The forestry authority wanted *"total control"* over the national parks. *"The natives get in the way of their plans."*

Ullash Kumar can cite many examples of corrupt forestry officials: They take bribes for giving illegal lumbering concessions; they take bribes in exchange for acquiring special building permits for rich, big-city businesspeople and politicians so they can build exclusive mansions in the protected buffer zone areas of the national parks. The Indian press regularly reports on cases where parks officials have been involved in poaching activities, earning money from the illegal sale of the tigers they are meant to be protecting.

Ullash Kumar is convinced that the WWF shares responsibility for the dark side of India's tiger policy: *"It designed the Indian tiger policy that led to the resettlement of the Adivasi; it supports eco-tourism – things that harm tigers and other animals. I have many friends who've found a job with the WWF. If you're a biologist looking for work in India, there's no way around the WWF. In my experience the WWF does do good, but the bad it does outweighs it. The WWF has a hidden agenda. What concerns me the most is that the WWF lets corporations finance its tiger campaign. In this way the WWF becomes the henchman of powers that take no real interest in the forest dwellers or the tigers. I'm afraid that the real goal of such companies, in the long-term, is to use the national parks to get at the land."*

The establishment of national parks does, in fact, often resemble a modern form of land grab. Much more than just a safe haven for wild animals, the parks also harbor many valuable natural resources. The first step in the land grab process is to divest the indigenous tribes of their property rights. What was traditionally commonly owned land is then lost, becoming a commercial commodity. As a rule, national parks are publicly owned; the commercial exploitation of forest resources, however, is left to private companies and NGOs that make a profit out of it.

Tour operators are doing a swift business with eco-tourism, and the pharmaceutical and food multinationals are busy plundering the genetic reservoirs of the ancient forests; they want to collect and apply the data before most species have become extinct. The WWF is frequently at the negotiation table when the rights to the natural genetic resources of the rainforests are being divvied up. The organization advocates for profit-sharing agreements for the indigenous peoples, with the declared aim of integrating them in the global economy.

The expulsion of indigenous peoples from the core zones of the reserves creates a steady supply of cheap labor for the industrial mining and farming operations on the periphery of the forests. Very few of the expelled natives find jobs in the tourism industry. Most conservation refugees across the globe end up like Muthamma and her tribespeople, as modern-day slaves on the plantations that have sprung up on the outskirts of the world's remaining rainforests. Global capitalism is cutting into increasingly large forest areas in the Southern Hemisphere – often in the name of nature conservancy.

That evening we said our goodbyes to the honey gatherers. In the case of Muthamma it was to be a final farewell. A few months after our meeting, Ullash Kumar delivered the sad news that the clever, charismatic Adivasi tribal leader had died of kidney failure.

4. Fishy Friends

In the 1980s the WWF decided it wanted to be more than just a conservation organization, advocating for the world's big, beloved superstar animals. Taking a new, ecological tack the organization set out to protect nature from the fundamental evils of modern times. In a speech to celebrate the 20th anniversary of the WWF, founder Max Nicholson defined the enemy precisely: *"These are the giants: ruthless and harmful technological development; profligate waste of the world's readily available energy reserves; and senseless multiplication like crazy rabbits. The sad truth is that someone will have to tackle those three big nasties, and if it isn't to be us, who will?"*[4]

In its mission statement from late 1989 the WWF first began to speak of the *"sustainable use of renewable resources"* – this was the only way the planet's biodiversity and natural environment could be saved in the face of human overpopulation. Under the presidency of Prince Philip (1981–1996) the WWF developed into a global environmental organization that also regularly collaborated with global corporations. The panda had bedded down with profit, and soon a common strategic project was born: the *"green economy"*. A strategy for our times, bringing tidings of comfort and joy in the midst of climate collapse and rainforest decimation: there would be more growth and more consumerism while simultaneously conserving natural resources – on land and in the water.

In the past, whenever I saw the likable little WWF panda on a poster, a soup packet or a beer can, my emotional response was largely positive – a result of the successful marketing that has made the WWF panda one of the world's most trusted brand logos. It was only by chance that I first ran across a story that would eventually shake my personal panda faith to the core. In the Steintor district of Bremen I ran into Luisa Ludwig, an old friend from Chile who I hadn't seen in years. After Pinochet's military putsch Luisa had lived in exile in Germany, and later returned home to teach at the German school in Santiago. She told me she now ran a little guesthouse in a tiny southern Chilean town with the melodious name of Puyuhuapi. There was nothing there, she said, but mountains, glaciers, fjords and several salmon farms in which a total environmental collapse had occurred. She said an estimated 100 million salmon had met an excruciating end in their huge underwater cages. At first it appeared they had been victims of the deadly salmon virus ISA, for which there is no cure. As it turned out, the real cause of the disaster was the greed of the salmon industry, in particular the Norwegian company Marine Harvest. My curiosity piqued, I searched the Internet and was astonished to find that John Fredriksen, one of the world's most infamous financial investors, is the principal owner of the company.

On the Marine Harvest website I not only found images of healthy-looking pink salmon and the company promise that it took its *"social and ecological responsibility"* very seriously, but also the friendly panda from the WWF. The pairing struck me as obscene – and the story certainly seemed interesting enough to be worth pursuing. In February 2009 I set off with my colleague Arno

Schumann on a journey to the end of the world. We wanted to get to the bottom of the fish farming disaster, and to find out how the panda had hooked up with the salmon.

From Santiago we took off on the new privately owned freeway for a 1,000-kilometer road trip down to the cold south. I had been there for the first time in 1981 and remembered the region as a green paradise, with dark forests, snow-dusted volcanic mountains and deep, blue lakes. But the forests south of Valdivia had now been completely replaced by pulp plantations: slender, brown-green pines and eucalyptus trees lined up in rigid rows like soldiers. Between the rows of trees were wide muddy aisles plowed up by the mechanical harvesters.

Every few years the industrial tree crops are felled, stripped bare in seconds, and transported to one of the gigantic pulp mills nearby – their belching smokestacks can be seen from kilometers away. What remains is a landscape that is naked, industrially standardized and biologically dead. The forest sell-out had been the brainchild of the Chicago Boys, a group of economists that obliged the Pinochet dictatorship with tips on the quickest way to turn Chile's rich natural resources into cold hard cash.

Oddly enough, many of these pulp lumber operations now bear the "ecolabel" FSC, which stands for Forest Stewardship Council, co-founded by the WWF. This certification has a good reputation for enforcing especially strict standards – companies who bare the label practice *"sustainable"* lumber production only. That, at any rate, is the claim of the FSC, an NGO with its headquarters in Bonn, Germany. The Shell oil company, a major financial sponsor of the WWF, also runs enormous tree plantations in southern Chile, as well as in Argentina and Paraguay. Shell, too, has received the squeaky green FSC ecolabel for *"sustainable forestry"*. The certification eases business dealings, but also the conscience of customers.

The idea of the FSC founders had originally been to enable natural forests to be exploited in a genuinely sustainable manner, preserving and protecting them for the future. But the fact is that a majority of the wood now bearing the FSC label comes from industrial plantations that are little more than green deserts, devoid of diverse plant and animal life. The few extreme survivalist organisms that do manage to hang on in these wastelands are snuffed out with herbicides and pesticides.

The Salmon King

Nearing the city of Puerto Montt we were met with the stench of rotten fish. It wasn't the salmon farms that stank but the fishmeal factories. They produce the feed for the voracious aquaculture fish, which are quickly fattened for the slaughter, gaining 5 kilograms within 18 months, a feat that can only be achieved with feed concentrates made of fishmeal and fish oil.

The smell followed us all the way to the ferry terminal at the port of Pargua, where we caught the ferry to Chiloé Island. Back in 1981 I had visited this fabulously beautiful island, with its seaside pile dwellings and enduring water spirit folklore. It was a poor but beautiful place. It was now barren and ugly, and the people still poverty-stricken, in spite of the *"salmon miracle"*.

The huge steel rings of the salmon cages could be seen in the fjords, in stark contrast to the blue of the water; container trucks jammed the highways. The red containers carried a toxic freight: millions of salmon carcasses contaminated with the virus. They had been slaughtered and were now being taken to the fishmeal factories for disposal. There they would be made into feed pellets for their surviving salmon brethren – recycling, Chilean style. The virulent salmon disease ISA has been an ecological disaster. At the time of our visit most of the salmon farms had already been shut down by the authorities and put under quarantine for a number of years.

Achao was a grim place. The rain had been falling for hours onto the rooftops, shingled with gray alerce wood. The seafood restaurants were empty; a few drunken men in Marine Harvest rain jackets staggered down the street towards us. On the shore two old women sat under a wooden shelter selling hand-knitted socks and sweaters to feed their families – the men had been fired without notice when ISA broke out. The company had given them two months severance pay – the equivalent of 550 dollars.

Maria, one of the women, complained: *"The industry promised us prosperity but the salmon have brought only misfortune. My husband and our three sons are now out of work. They can't go back to working as fishermen; there's nothing more to fish: no mussels, no sea urchins, everything's dead."* When I asked whom she thought was responsible for the disaster she said: *"The Norwegians. They made a lot of money with the salmon. Now that they've contaminated our ocean they're just clearing off."*

A third of all commercial salmon production worldwide is in the hands of the Norwegian John Fredriksen. With an estimated private fortune of 13.5 billion dollars the corpulent, ruddy-faced *"salmon king"* is one of the richest men on the planet. Fredriksen started out as a small herring merchant, and the Norwegian bourgeoisie still see him as a parvenu with crude manners. His motto is simple: *"Anything that's good for the shareholders is good for the company."* He jets around the world on his razzias accompanied by a small entourage of 18 staff members.

Whenever a business that Fredriksen deems strategically important falters he moves in, buying up stocks until he has a controlling share of the company. Fredrik-

"King Salmon", John Fredriksen (on the right)

sen has used this modus operandi to amass a substantial global empire: he owns Frontline, the world's largest tanker fleet, and Seadrill, the market leader in oil platforms. John Fredriksen got into the salmon trade more or less by chance. In 2007 a major Norwegian salmon company was about to go bankrupt. Fredriksen bought it and then merged with two other players in that fishy business. Since then he's been the big daddy of the salmon industry as well. His aquaculture company Marine Harvest dumps 100 million salmon a year onto the global market. Aquaculture professes to be a *"clean"* method of producing fish in large quantities. The WWF has elected to do a partnership deal with Fredriksen's company – presumably because the organization believes that intensive farming in the sea is the solution to the food supply problems of the future.

Swimming Pharmacies

On a boat ride through the Reloncaví Fjord a few kilometers south of Puerto Montt, marine biologist Héctor Kol described the farm-bred salmon as *"swimming pharmacies"*. With 38 salmon and trout farms located in the fjord, its capacities are maxed out. An average of 200,000 salmon are crammed into each cage – twice as many as permitted in Europe. A single Chilean farm with six cages thus stocks over a million fish at any given time. The individual farms are much too close together; infectious disease can spread in a flash: the virus epidemic was a disaster waiting to happen.

A year earlier there had been a mass salmon "jailbreak" in the Reloncaví Fjord that saw 130,000 salmon on the loose. Salmon are predators, and the escapees had soon gobbled up everything in the fjord; there was nothing left for the local fishermen to catch. Héctor Kol knows every salmon farm in the area; he used to be a project developer for the industry, until he realized that his work was contributing to ecosystem collapse in the fjords. He quit his job, and has worked for a pittance consulting the small-scale fishermen's cooperatives ever since. Throughout southern Chile, wherever there is a salmon workers' strike or a blockade staged by outraged fishermen, the wiry high-strung chain smoker can't be far away: Héctor Kol is a man on a mission.

Héctor Kol, salmon rebel

The salmon industry views Kol as a ringleader and a traitor – he has to watch his back. Environmental activists from Santiago had warned him of a possible attempt on his life, but Héctor Kol was a hardened veteran of the resistance against the Pinochet dictatorship: *"I won't stop until the salmon dictatorship in Chile is over as well."* As we drove along the bumpy fjordside sand roads he pointed to the white silos on the shore: *"There are too many salmon in the cages, so there's not enough oxygen, and they suffocate."* The silos were oxygen compressors used to give artificial respiration to the sea.

Héctor Kol had taken samples at many different farms – always with the salmon company security boats hot on his heels. He had also studied the companies' environmental reports in detail: *"In Norway it is permissible to use one gram of antibiotics per ton of salmon produced; in Chile there are no restrictions. Here they sometimes use up to eight hundred times the amount of antibiotics as in Europe – the same antibiotics that are used to treat humans. That's dangerous, because the bacteria become resistant to them. In one year Marine Harvest added as much antibiotics to the feed at a single farm in this fjord than used by the entire Norwegian salmon industry that same year."*

In addition to the antibiotics, other dangerous chemical substances are also used to push salmon production volumes higher still. Héctor Kol knows them all: *"Even the salmon eggs are treated with fungicides, which contain carcinogenic substances such as crystal violet and malachite green. The feeding cages are routinely painted with antifouling agents that contain heavy metals."*

The marine biologist opened his laptop and showed us video footage shot by a mussel diver of the seabed beneath the salmon farm cages. An undersea garbage landscape unfolded on the screen: pipes, old fishing nets and parts of cages, rotten feed and a thick layer of salmon feces, with dead mussels, sea urchins and starfish floating in the murky soup. *"Everything's been killed off down there. The industry uses the sea as a garbage dump; the salmon in our farms produce the same amount of feces as the 14 million inhabitants of Chile. The entire marine ecosystem is being ruthlessly destroyed for a quick profit – and the WWF is doing nothing to stop it."*

When Panda Met Salmon

What the WWF did do was to enter into a partnership agreement with Marine Harvest, in April 2008. The press release announcing the collaboration said the two parties were joining forces to advance the production of *"sustainable"* salmon. To Héctor Kol that sounded like a cynical sneer: *"25,000 workers have already lost their jobs because half of the aquaculture farms have had to close down due to the virus pandemic. Where is the social sustainability the WWF talks about? It claims that the salmon industry is good for Chile, which is just stabbing us in the back."* I offered that the dialogue between the WWF and the company had its positive aspects. There had been small improvements. For example, the Chilean WWF and Adolfo Alvial, the Technical Director of Marine Harvest in Chile, had planned a pilot project: in future the young salmon, called smolt, would be kept in closed tanks while they grew, so they would no longer soil the fjords and lakes. Héctor dismissed my argument: *"That's just a token initiative. Where are those tanks? They exist only on paper; Marine Harvest isn't going to spend a single Peso on them."*

The following day we went to meet with Marine Harvest Chile director Adolfo Alvial. He admitted outright that the water tank project had, in fact, been *"suspended"*. The company currently had other, more pressing,

Salmon farm in Chile

concerns: "*We've also been hit very hard by the virus crisis. We'll take up the idea again when the time is ripe. The WWF appreciates our position.*" Alvial proved to be one of the company's self-critical thinkers. As a biologist he was well aware that the industry had inflicted serious damage to the ecosystem of the Chilean fjords: "*We've made many mistakes, but we, and John Fredriksen personally, are determined to learn from them. It is possible to reconcile sustainability with profit. We can't give up now, because we have a responsibility for feeding humankind. The small-scale independent fishermen can't catch enough; we need aquaculture.*"

The crisis in Chile has led to a salmon shortage on the world market, triggering a rise in prices. Marine Harvest has responded by ramping up production in Norway. In Chile the company has behaved like a vulture circling above the dying industry: as smaller companies succumb to the epidemic Marine Harvest has moved in to buy up their infrastructure. When the crisis is over Fredriksen will have even more control over the global salmon trade than before the outbreak. And the extermination of millions of diseased salmon won't put the company in the red – the fish were well insured.

Outside a McDonald's in Oslo advertising banners fluttered in the wind. The omnipresent American eatery was promoting its latest creation: the new Marine Harvest salmon wrap, with which Fredriksen hoped to penetrate new markets, winning over young urbane consumers with a hip *"sustainable"* product.

We were in Oslo to meet with Maren Esmark, Marine Conservation Officer at WWF Norway. She had negotiated the partnership deal with Marine Harvest. I questioned her about the ethics of cooperating with a company that is clearly a two-faced beast: in Norway it seems to behave properly, and at the same time it's destroying marine ecosystems and people's lives in Chile. Ms. Esmark responded with unruffled diplomacy: *"The partnership with Marine Harvest is still young and only applies to Norway. The situation in Chile is unfortunate, but Chile is not part of our partnership agreement."* How convenient! Never mind that it's one and the same company. That's what I call double-dealing. I was starting to get on Maren Esmark's nerves: *"What exactly do you want? We could stop the dialogue with Marine Harvest, but do you think that would make the world a better place?"*

She firmly believed that the partnership with the WWF had already made Marine Harvest *"better"*, at least in Norway. Together they would continue to *"reduce the company's ecological footprint"*. New measures would be introduced, for example to prevent so many salmon from escaping their cages. Because when the aquafarmed salmon breeds with wild varieties, genetic diversity is lost. The WWF also aimed to use the partnership to solve the problem of salmon feed. The company fed its stocks, in Norway as well, on a mixture containing North Sea herring. The plan was to replace this popular seafood, wherever possible, with protein from fish considered inedible by humans.

I pressed the point: did the partnership agreement include binding commitments? Who monitors the company to make sure it keeps its promises? The WWF representative remained vague: *"At the moment it's about testing the waters and formulating joint, verifiable goals in the partnership."* Fed up with the corporate-speak, I asked to see a copy of the agreement. Maren Esmark was unable to oblige: *"The agreement is being revised at Marine Harvest. I'll send you a copy as soon as it's finished."* She did not. Several subsequent requests also failed to produce the document; I never did get to see it. Perhaps it was really more of a non-bonding declaration of intent than an actual credible contract. That would certainly be a cost-effective way for the company to *"green"* its tarnished image.

But what was in it for the WWF? Was money changing hands? A rather uncomfortable question for Maren Esmark, who hesitated before answering: *"Yes, the agreement also involves money. We get financial support for our work on marine conservation."* When I asked how much money Fredriksen's empire funnels into the WWF, she looked searchingly around for help but there was no one to come to her aid. *"Well, it's ... in euro or in Norwegian crowns?"* – *"The currency makes no difference."* – *"Okay.*

Well, the WWF gets about 100,000 euros a year." That's almost 135,000 dollars. Per annum.

Did she think it was a case of: *"He who pays the piper calls the tune"*? Oddly, Maren Esmark was quick to agree, albeit by putting a new spin on an old saying: *"Yes, every partnership with industrial companies is a challenge. But as a global organization we have to come to terms with that. We work with large companies while at the same time criticizing them, regardless of whether we are taking their money."*

Then why wasn't the WWF criticizing the ecological misdeeds of its partner in Chile? *"That is outside of WWF Norway's purview."* But this excuse had apparently been forgotten only minutes later when Maren Esmark launched into a fervent plea of support for the Chilean operations: *"We believe that the salmon industry will bring great benefit to Chile's coastal inhabitants. It creates jobs and pay and we don't want that to stop."*

Death in a Cage

Cristián Soto is one of 50,000 people employed in the Chilean salmon industry. His job as a diver takes him down to the icy depths of the salmon cages. The WWF is not in his good books. He wonders why the organization does nothing for the people who work and die for Marine Harvest. He, too, risks his life daily for the salmon business. As a day laborer on the aquaculture farms of Marine Harvest and other operators he cleans and repairs nets and removes the contaminated carcasses of diseased salmon. At the time of our meeting that was about 3,000 dead salmon a day – per cage: *"There are not enough transport containers available so we have to pack the dead salmon in sacks, which are left hanging in the cages until a ship comes by to collect them. By that time the salmon are already decomposing and the stench is horrific. We do all of this work without any protective clothing whatsoever."*

Christián Soto, diver

We rented a little fishing boat and chugged along with Cristián Soto to visit a sea lion colony on the other side of the fjord. Almost a hundred of the imposing animals were sunning themselves there on the rocks. The bulls, which weigh over a ton, roared fearsomely as we approached. The sea lion is a protected species in Chile but the salmon companies continue to hunt them mercilessly nonetheless: sea lions love salmon. One of Cristián Soto's jobs is to chase the sea lions out of the cages. *"When they manage to get into a cage we have to get them out. First they shoot them; usually the operations manager does that. Then we have to go down to see if they're really dead – it's a life-threatening job. You can refuse to do it, but then they say: don't bother showing up here tomorrow. Last year a sea lion injured by a gunshot got ahold of my leg and pulled me down into deep water. My fins and mask were torn off in the process. I survived."*

The lives of the around 6,000 salmon divers in Chile hang on a sort of garden hose that supplies them with air from above. The tubes are often damaged and prone to tearing. Sometimes the divers also get tangled up in the nets down below and can't get back up to the surface. The water pressure is immense, because the divers have to go down much further than the legal limit. *"Our license only permits us to dive a maximum of 20 meters deep, but the cages are 40 meters down. The law states that every salmon farm must have a decompression chamber within a radius of 500 meters; that's a matter of life and death when it comes to a diving accident. In reality they don't exist, or they're defective. A dead diver is cheaper for the company. 18 of my colleagues lost their lives last year alone."*

One of them was one of Cristián Soto's best friends: *"It took seven hours to get him to the next operable decompression chamber. He was dead on arrival."* The diver told us the story with tears in his eyes; death was his constant companion. Why did he subject himself to it? He's actually a music teacher, but you can't live on a teacher's salary in Chile. *"I do it so that my two children can go to a good school."* The divers make good money by Chilean standards: about 1,200 euros a month.

Cristián invited us back to his home, opened a computer database and showed us the picture of a young colleague who had lost his life on August 26th 2007 on the Marine Harvest farm Puchilco. Cristián read us a passage from the accident investigator's report: *"The diver had no valid license. Damage to the equipment prevented him from being supplied with oxygen. The compulsory rescue diver was not present."*

The dead diver was Pedro Pablo Alvarado. He was 29 when he lost his life at a depth of 40 meters, where he was repairing the nets that guard against sea lions. Cristián had studied the files of the public prosecution and spoken with colleagues and bereaved relatives: *"The company claims that the accident happened at a depth of 20 meters – that's the maximum depth he was legally allowed to dive to with his license. Everyone knows that can't be the case, because the sea lion nets hang at a depth of 40 meters. Furthermore: Pedro Pablo had to dive during a storm, although the Marines, as the responsible authority, had prohibited all diving in the area."*

I inquired at the relevant public prosecution department about the outcome of the investigation: two years after the diver's death Marine Harvest had had to pay a fine of ca. 2,700 dollars – for violation of safety regulations. The public prosecutor had declined to pursue a charge of involuntary manslaughter. The justice system protects the perpetrators, not the victims, according to Cristián Soto: *"Every time there's an accident the public prosecutor comes to the same conclusion: the only one responsible for the death is the diver himself. The criminal justice system doesn't protect us. That is very unjust. I've been lucky up to now. But my family has to get used to the idea that one day I won't come back either."*

This story illustrates that the salmon industry is prepared to rationalize the loss of divers' lives in the name of efficiency. In the language of economics it's the *"comparative cost advantage"* that northern countries have when

Divers with salmon carcasses

they relocate their operations to the south. In the past ten years, an estimated 100 Chilean divers have died in the cages. In the Norwegian salmon industry there was one diver death in the same period. We decided to confront the company with these numbers. Adolfo Alvial, the Marine Harvest Technical Director in Chile, was willing to talk to us, but he first wanted to show us his pride and joy: the new eco breeding farm Rio Blanco, located in the gentle rolling foothills of the Andes. It is the most modern installation of its kind: clean, environmentally friendly, with closed-circuit water systems and biofilters. Here, in huge tubs, was the new generation of farm-bred salmon – all 10 million of them.

What a contrast to the company's brutal salmon cage habitats! I remarked on this difference to Alvial and told him I felt like Alice in Wonderland. He gave a satisfied smile: *"You're in reality. Chile is the land of wonders. This facility shows the change of course that Marine Harvest is making. This is where we want to go, although there's still a lot to be done."*

Next question: why did 100 divers have to die to keep the salmon business booming? The suave smile suddenly vanished from Adolfo's face: *"There is no explanation for that. I could argue with the number 100. Sometimes the victims are mussel divers who dive along the coast at their own risk, and when they get killed it's blamed on us. That's unfair. But never mind that, even if it's only 10, 12 or 20: every death is one too many."* As soon as our camera was shut off he leaned over and said with a wink: *"Just between us, most of the divers die because they come to work drunk. Their archenemy is alcohol, not the company."*

Petter's Happy Salmon

Back again to Norway, where we met with Marine Harvest's Technical Director, Petter Arnesen. A sincere, reserved man, who led us to his speedboat, in which we would view with him the model living conditions of the corporation's Norwegian salmon. The head of PR had just resigned and management had foisted the task on Arnesen – he had negotiated the partnership agreement with the WWF, after all. The global *"Aquaculture Dialogue"* program was another brainchild of Arnesen and the WWF. It would issue new sustainability certification to enable the global aquaculture industry to shed its grubby image once and for all.

Petter Arnesen admitted that, to date, agreements with the WWF had been imprecise and generalized. The actual documentation was still *"in flux"*. The most important thing, however, was the ongoing dialogue: *"We learn something from the WWF about marine ecological processes, and the WWF can learn how aquaculture really works."* And Marine Harvest's payments to the WWF? What were they for, exactly? According to Arnesen the money goes to finance the post of WWF salmon expert. He saw nothing objectionable about a company paying the salary of its external critics. Not least because of the disaster in Chile, Marine Harvest would have to become *"more sustainable"* to survive. That's where the WWF could help. In Norway, said Petter Arnesen, everything was already much better than in the Chilean operations anyway.

We seemed to fly in the boat across the dark green waters of the Bokna Fjord. Along the steep banks waterfalls crashed from great heights into the sea below. Every few kilometers huge rings could be seen rising from the water: salmon farms. Automatic feeding machines hurled feed pellets into the air and immediately thousands of salmon breached the surface to snap them up. Their scaly bodies glistened in the sunlight. With utter sincerity, Technical Director Arnesen ensured us that his salmon were *"absolutely happy"*.

The contrast to Chile was clearly evident: the water in the Norwegian aquafarming areas is barely sullied; hygiene regulations are adhered to, and state supervision is strict. Violators of environmental laws lose the licensing that operators In Norway must reapply for annually, for every farm. Marine Harvest gets its Chilean licenses at a rock bottom price: 150 dollars a year for one hectare of sea area. And then there are the low wages in Chile: about ten percent of labor costs in Norway.

One company, two completely different sets of standards. Petter Arnesen admitted that with the Chilean operations there had been a big temptation to start turning a quick profit right away, and that: *"We should have seen that the disaster was inevitable."* Because several years prior, there had already been an ISA outbreak in Norway. But because the salmon farms there are farther apart and the hygiene standards higher, they had managed to stop the spread of the virus within a few months, whereas in Chile the epidemic raged as far south as the Strait of Magellan, extending its reach across 1000 kilometers. Petter Arnesen shares personal responsibility for the catastrophe; he spent years in Chile helping to establish the salmon aquafarming industry there. *"Yes,"* he admitted reluctantly, *"unfortunately we hadn't learned enough from the lesson we'd been taught in Norway."* He slumped down a bit and stared silently ahead for a few seconds before adding: *"I think it would have been better if you had submitted your questions before the interview."*

As soon as he had composed himself again, Arnesen proclaimed in a firm voice that all of the challenges in aquaculture would be mastered, including the biggest one of all: how to convert salmon to vegetarianism? The carnivorous predator fish need large amounts of animal protein. The feed concentrate dumped into the cages by the ton is made mainly of fishmeal and fish oil. It's a negative cycle: 4–6 kilograms of wild fish are killed and made into meal to produce one kilo of salmon flesh. More than half of the world's fish catch now goes to making feed concentrate for salmon and other animals. Farm-bred salmon consume more animal protein than they produce. How can that be sustainable?

"We see the problem the same way the WWF does," conceded Petter Arnesen. "We're experimenting with increasing the share of vegetable protein in the feed, using soy, for example." The company was determined to achieve this, he said, as the fish reserves of the world's oceans were already *"exhausted"*. The trouble is, when there is too little fish product in the feed the salmon raised on it no longer contain as much healthy omega 3 fatty acids. That's not the kind of salmon the retailers want. The poor Technical Director has the daunting task of circling the square – luckily the WWF can lend him a hand: by simply designating the whole thing *"sustainable"*.

Could genetic engineering be the answer? Arnesen wisely kept quiet on the subject. The company wouldn't consider *"that sort of thing"*; it couldn't be *"communicated"* to European consumers. But in 2013, the time had come after all: in a laboratory on Prince Edward Island in Canada the US biotech company Aquabounty produced the first genetically modified salmon. The Canadian Ministry of the Environment had granted permission for the commercial mass production and marketing of the GM salmon eggs. The mood at Aquabounty was upbeat; they were confident that the US Food and Drug Administration (FDA) would soon approve the marketing of its whopping *"Frankenfish"*, which grows twice as fast as conventional farm-bred salmon. I feared that it, too, would soon bear the *"sustainable aquaculture"* seal of approval.

We could already smell the Chilean port city of Talcahuano miles before we reached it. The harbor of the fishmeal hub was lined with modern trawlers; the Humboldt current region off the coast of Chile is thought to have the most abundant fish stocks in the world. On the quay we met up with Nelson Estrada. After 19 hours out to sea in stormy weather, he and his 13 compadres were busy unloading 90 tons of fresh anchovies with a huge hose that reaches down into the hold like an elephant's trunk to suck up the catch. The fish are then taken by truck to one of the local fishmeal factories. It's always a bleak moment for Nelson Estrada: *"The industry has bought up most of the fishing licenses. Our entire catch goes to the feed industry – although anchovies are very healthy and high in protein. It's criminal. This industry disgusts me, but I have to support my family, that's why I work for them."*

Nelson is a fisherman's union activist and was in a hurry; the next morning the trawler crewmen would be going on strike to protest the low prices paid by the fishmeal factories for the fish. The captains weren't earning enough money to pay off the trawlers, which had been financed by the fishmeal factories, making captain and crew totally dependent on the feed industry: *"We're nothing but slaves of the transnational industry; there are no independent fishermen left in Chile."* Nelson Estrada is a born fisherman. At 12 he lost his father to the sea. He invited us on board and took us into the hold, where he showed us the multi-ton mountain of glistening little anchovy bodies: *"I'm ashamed of this here: these fish are tiny; they haven't even reached sexual maturity. We're plundering the stocks before they can even reproduce. There'll be nothing left for future generations."*

95 percent of all fish caught in Chilean waters end up as feed concentrate for salmon, pigs, cattle and chickens. They are the fuel for a greedy global intensive farming industry that is bringing the world to its knees. Nelson Estrada is a fighter, but he, too, felt that the economic cards were stacked hopelessly against him: *"Our government is too weak to stand up to the corporations. It's more convenient for the politicians to take sides with the powerful financial players, in the name of 'free-market economy'. They play along, but the rules are made by others."*

In with the Sharks

At the far corner of the salmon empire Douglas Tompkins is lord of the land. His personal national park Pumalín lies nestled up against the Andes in Patagonia. Many Chilean conservationists don't trust him; in their view, Tompkins is a globalization *"profiteer"*. He had grown his own companies Esprit and The North Face into huge empires by moving production to low-wage Asian countries.

When I put the criticisms to him, Tompkins gave a weary smile: *"I don't deny it. But when it became clear to me where this type of globalization would lead, I took the consequences and got out."* He sold his shares in the enterprises and used the money to buy up one of the last temperate rainforests in Patagonia. He thus rescued a green paradise of 290,000 hectares from the chainsaws of the pulp industry. Tompkins is now regarded by the worldwide nature conservation movement as something of a *"deep ecology"* guru. Not satisfied with cosmetic corrections, this movement advocates putting a complete stop to the obsession with unchecked growth. Tompkins has no sympathy for the way the WWF cozies up to industry: *"The idea that there can be sustainable intensive farming in the ocean is crazy; it's a dangerous illusion that brings us closer to ecological collapse."*

Douglas Tompkins

When Tompkins started his project here 20 years ago he never suspected that he would one day be hemmed in by industrial aquaculture. The gaunt, delicate man with the lucent eyes sat facing me in an armchair in his old, restored villa – a wooden palace right on the shore of Lake Llanquihue. The Gringo, as he's called here, is constantly at loggerheads with his neighbors the salmon farms. They put his paradise at risk; he maddens them by filing charges whenever they break the already lenient Chilean environmental laws. For example when one of the local farms installed 24 cages – twice as many as permitted.

Was he glad that nature was now striking back at the hubris of the aquaculture industry in the form of the salmon virus? A friendly smile spread across Tompkins's face and it looked as though he would nod in agreement, but then suppressed the impulse: *"I can't be pleased about it, because the crisis left many people destitute. I do care about them. Still, they should use the opportunity to just shut down the salmon industry. Traditional fishing practices are much better; they can be done in an organic, sustainable manner. Chile is a paradise for fish and shellfish. Many more people could be employed in the traditional fishing industry than in salmon farming, and they would live with much more dignity."*

The rampant corporate growth, he said, was like a *"ferocious acceleration machine"* that would destroy everything beautiful on the planet. The situation in Chile illustrated that *"Karl Marx was right: capitalism devours itself in the end"*. Tompkins said he believed the WWF dialogue policy to be a strategic misconception: *"The destruction of the planet can be stopped only by the civil resistance that exists in Chile, and in many other countries on Earth. These grass roots movements have joined together to become an increasingly powerful force."*

The rich American feared that Chile's political class didn't have the strength to seize the opportunity and reverse the trend. On the contrary, they were now planning to open up the untouched glacial region in the south of the Magellan Strait to the relentless "Forward, march!" of global capitalism. There were plans for a highway that would extend all the way down to Punta Arenas, and five huge hydroelectric plants were also in the works. The energy from these facilities would enable corporations from the US, Canada, and Europe to finally crack open the glaciers and mountains to get at the mother lode within.

The salmon industry, too, stood in the starting blocks for the southward sprint: the government had already issued the first licenses for new aquafarms in the southern Magellan Strait. According to Tompkins, the companies were advancing like a swarm of locusts, leaving a trail of destruction in their wake: "*With industrial fish farming we are producing a dead planet. There's no economic diversity anymore, just like there's no longer any diversity out there in the ocean. They reduce everything down to a single species: salmon. This development will catch up with us one day, and we'll pay for it, because we've forgotten that we're a part of nature. Let nature manage the oceans. She knows how; she's proved it for billions of years. Businessmen like John Fredriksen believe that as long as the profit's good everything else will take care of itself. The opposite is true.*"

Pandas Don't Bite

At the end of our voyage through the realm of the salmon we finally located the monarch himself: a solitary John Fredriksen stood wearing angler's hat and raingear in the little river of Naustdal in central Norway, angling for wild salmon. He loves the peace and quiet there more than anything and leases an entire section of the river, where now he alone is allowed to fish. He comes to his private piece of river once or twice during the season – no one knows the exact dates. I had taken my daughter along and rented rooms in a nearby farmhouse for two weeks, speculating on the arrival of Big John. Just as we were about to give up and head home, and were making a last riverside surveillance round, we saw smoke rising from the chimney of Fredriksen's little smokehouse. Someone had fired up the fish-smoking oven. From a deeply mistrustful villager I was able to coax the information that Fredriksen had arrived early that morning – airlifted in by his personal helicopter.

Concealed in the bushes along the riverbank we observed him through binoculars. He was waiting for a salmon to bite. No luck; there were no salmon there to take the bait. Even in that exclusive Norwegian salmon Shangri-la their stocks have been decimated by the parasites, bacteria, and viruses unleashed on the wild populations by the aquafarms. When the wild salmon come from the open sea and swim upstream to their river spawning grounds they pass by the farms and become infected by their captive relatives. They die of the disease before getting a chance to spawn the next generation.

In a silent burst of anger, John Fredriksen threw his fishing rod into the bushes as I waded towards him in the shallows. He called for his bodyguards but the sound of the rushing waterfalls drowned out his voice. He had no choice but to stomp back towards his fishing villa. Soon afterwards his people came after me in a van to confiscate the film I had shot. We jumped into the car and made a quick getaway. What a shame! Fredriksen had missed the opportunity for an engaging conversation over smoked salmon and beer. I would have loved to have asked what motivates him and why he always has to be the biggest at

John Fredriksen in London

everything he does. Later on I made a final twilight attempt: I got his housekeeper on the phone, but she relayed the message that her employer wished no further contact.

Every other year John Fredriksen attends the Nor-Shipping maritime trade fair in Oslo. The biennial mega event week is considered the leading international industry show of its kind. For me it was the last chance to make personal contact; we searched all day in vain for Fredriksen. A Norwegian shipbroker consoled me: *"John is a shy guy, but I'm sure he'll be here tonight."* That evening was the night of the shipping magnates, with a VIP party on the celebrated tall ship Christian Radich – a champagne and caviar affair.

We set up our camera dockside of the three-masted venue and waited. Late that night we finally caught sight of Fredriksen's twin daughters as they clattered up the swaying gangway in black mini-dresses and high heels. Once on board, the future heiresses to a multi-billion fortune immediately attracted a whole flock of eager suitors. The young women are both already on the management boards of daddy's companies: Kathrine has a hand in shipping, Cecilie in salmon. The following night we were in luck: we finally caught the big fish by chance, in the middle of the Oslo harbor promenade.

My journalist colleague Arno Schumann made a beeline for Fredriksen, camera rolling. Fredriksen's companions closed ranks to protect him. I shouted through the human shield, asking if he felt personally responsible for the calamity that was still ravaging Chile. The salmon king continued on his way, po-faced, but then reacted after all with a little joke: *"I'm just a salmon fisher"*. When I reminded him that he owned Marine Harvest he immediately changed his tune and grew serious: *"I have nothing to do with the operational business, but I'm very sorry about what's happened. I sympathize with everyone there who has been affected."* Fredriksen then quickly disappeared into an upscale restaurant to enjoy a gourmet meal of fresh oysters, fish and fine wine. Anchors aweigh and off to new business opportunities. There was no Chilean salmon on the menu there that night.

Why would the WWF seek out someone like John Fredriksen, of all people, as a partner for saving the planet? He is the prototypical financial investor, obedient to the law of profit; the Earth's natural resources are apparently little more to him than the means to erecting his cold, monetary castle. Fredriksen could have gone down in the annals as one of the most notorious bad guys in the history of corporate capitalism. But then, as if by divine intervention, the panda had plopped down in his lap. And suddenly his empire took on a miraculous green glow.

Over half of the global fish catch now ends up in the mills of the fishmeal factories instead of on people's plates. As fish stocks worldwide become increasingly depleted, the salmon industry is turning to a new feed source. Companies have now begun to send huge trawlers into the Antarctic to fish for krill, the tiny crabs that are the oceans' staff of life; the largest nutritional reserves of the world's maritime systems. Krill, too, are now being used to make salmon feed.

Chilean aquafarmed salmon travel across the globe by airfreight, destined to land in bite-sized portions on restaurant tables in Paris, Tokyo, and New York, et al. The hungry diner sees only a perfectly innocent-looking delicate rosy-pink piece of fish. But the appearance of the salmon belies the martyrdom it has endured to end up there; the numerous chemicals and antibiotics it had to swallow to survive life in the crowded cages. And you can't tell by looking at the meal on the plate how much energy was used to produce it, and how much was wasted on long-distance shipment. For those at the top of the financial food chain, the bottom line makes it all worthwhile, but is the whole thing really socially and ecologically acceptable?

Intensive farming is accelerating the depletion of natural resources and destroying the traditional fishing industry. Thus *"sustainable salmon farming"* is a fairytale concocted by the aquafarming industry and the WWF in a collaboration aimed at lulling our critical thinking capacities to sleep. There is no right way to do the wrong thing. The big sharks eat everything that gets in their way. And the political authorities elected to represent the interests of civil society feebly allow the multinational corporations to make all the rules in the global game.

The WWF apparently swims with sharks in the audacious hope that its moral influence will turn them into docile vegetarians. In the summer of 2011, the WWF finally reached an agreement with the industrial salmon sector, and together they launched the certification program for marine farming facilities: the Aquaculture Stewardship Council, or ASC. With that, the intensive farming of fish in the open sea rose to the ranks of nobility in the realm of the green economy.

During my research for this book I also spoke with many WWF activists. They were committed to their area of interest and were certainly doing the best job they could; they knew very little about the WWF's international partnerships – and didn't want to hear anything about them either. However, when confronted with the fact that the world's oceans are being fished bare to feed a predator species in intensive aquafarming units, they did at least seem to suspect that all could not be completely rosy. The typical reaction was, in effect: *"I really don't want to know all the gory details. My own project is above board, and that's what I'm concentrating on."*

A management-level staffer at WWF International told me in confidence that he was *"ashamed"* of the partnership with the salmon industry, but a public airing of his critical views was out of the question; it would certainly cost him his well-paid job. This individual said the loss of *"credibility"* in WWF policies was down to sociological developments: the WWF had grown too big, and collected money without making sure they knew where it came from. The classic environmentalists had been *"ousted"* from executive positions in the WWF and replaced by marketing specialists who failed to take a *"principled"* stance on nature conservation issues and saw themselves primarily as fundraisers.

The critical thinkers within the WWF are deeply frustrated, but to date the internals conflicts that are presumably smoldering have been successfully kept under wraps. In Germany, for example, many WWF activists have for many years taken part in protests against nuclear energy – but strictly as private individuals, displaying no visible WWF affiliation. Not until 2002 did WWF International officially distance itself from nuclear energy production, finally joining the growing ranks of atomic energy phase-out proponents.

Can the proximity of the WWF to big business be explained by the lure of money and recognition alone? A former WWF manager who left over ethical issues but would like to remain anonymous suspects there is more to it than the increasing dependency on major donations. In her view: *"The WWF is like a pizzeria. Everything looks clean and nice on the outside. And they actually do have pizza – delicious, made from certified organic ingredients. But this pizzeria has a back room where all the really important deals are done – that frightens me."*

5. It All Began in Africa

To really understand the WWF and its political role, you must go deep down into the catacombs of the British Empire, the demise of which gained momentum in the 1950s and 1960s with the loss of almost all the African colonies. Africa is the birthplace of the WWF. The prologue to its story began in the year 1940, when Great Britain declared the Serengeti the first national park in East Africa – an area the size of Northern Ireland. The colonial authority had made the plan palatable to London on the basis of two arguments: there were no major mineral deposits in the Serengeti; and the terrain was unattractive for European settlers – it didn't rain enough and there were too many tsetse flies. The Serengeti would become a *"worldwide tourism sensation"*.

The only problem was: the Massai, the indigenous tribal people who for centuries had lived with their cattle herds in the Serengeti. The British decided to legally guarantee them the right to remain – they were only herdsmen after all; they didn't work the land or hunt protected animals. The Massai were relieved. But they hadn't reckoned with the Western conservationists and the white park rangers who had nothing but disdain for the natives. Many tourists also complained about the sight of the *"dirty"* Massai and their *"barbaric ways"*. In the 1950s the colonial authorities introduced a new policy, offering the Massai the option of voluntary resettlement. But the tribal chiefs rejected the offer. Where else would there be so much wonderful grazing land and rivers to water the cattle? And wasn't it their land and that of their forefathers anyway?

The conservationists ramped up the pressure, which prompted the colonial administration of the Tanganyika Territory to take a Solomonic decision: the Serengeti National Park would be reduced from 5,000 to 1,800 square miles. The Massai would then have to leave the smaller park. A storm of protest was unleashed in Europe and the USA. It would soon develop into a tornado for the British colonial authority, when German wildlife conservationist Bernhard Grzimek got involved. He showed the world how a radical PR campaign could force a political about-face. Through his Serengeti mission the celebrated director of the Frankfurt Zoo became the ideological role model of modern nature conservancy – and the WWF.

Grzimek's Mission

Prof. Bernhard Grzimek flew with his son Michael over the Serengeti to observe the migrations of the big game animals. He published the results in his 1956 book 'No Place for Wild Animals'. It contains such apocalyptical declarations as *"Africa's wild animals are doomed to extinction"* with no scientific evidence to back his claims. According to Grzimek, too many people lived in the Serengeti, and the forests and steppes would be transformed into deserts because of it. He was convinced that pastoral tribes inherently destroy the ecosystems in which they live. A gross misconception, as prominent scientists of the day could have told him. Conservationist David

Western for example, who lived in Kenya and had spent many years studying the Massai, had come to the conclusion that: *"The herdsmen are actually the reason that there are still so many wild animals here."*[5] But the ignorance of outsiders was mightier than the experience of experts on site.

Bernhard Grzimek on a stamp

In 1959 Bernhard Grzimek followed up with the bestseller: 'Serengeti Shall Not Die'. The book was translated into 17 languages and served son Michael as the template for a film of the same name, which promptly received an Oscar nomination. The Grzimeks' main message: If we want to save the Serengeti, the Massai have to go. Nature as a human-free zone – no one formulated and propagated this mantra of an elite Western Nature apotheosis better and more incisively than the Frankfurt Zoo director. Grzimek concealed his racist-tinged views behind the stilted vocabulary of the well-meaning: *"We Europeans must teach our black brothers to value their own possessions, not because we are older or cleverer, but because we do not want them to repeat our mistakes and sins."*[6] The general public and Hollywood applauded, and the British colonial administration tried – shortly before the launch of 'Serengeti Shall Not Die' – to pull its head out of the noose.

In 1958 the colonial authorities submitted a declaration to the Massai chiefs for their signature. It stated that they and their people would agree to leave the Serengeti Park *"voluntarily"*. 30 years later, Raymond Bonner, a New York Times reporter, tracked down one of the few surviving signatories: Tendemo ole Kisaka. The old man told Bonner how the *"signing"* of the contract had gone down: *"We were told to sign. It was not explained to us. None of the tribal leaders could read or write."* The old man then added, grinning *"You white people are very tough."*[7]

A people that had lived in the Serengeti for 4,000 years was expelled – a cruel and bloody operation in which 100,000 Massai lost their homeland. From faraway London a tight group of aristocratic big game hunters-cum-nature-conservationists looked on with approval as the German zoo director carried out his plan. Grzimek's sweeping Serengeti campaign presumably inspired the elite old boys' club to come up with their own, much bigger project: the WWF – a sort of international avant-garde advocating for the wilderness.

Most indigenous tribal languages have no word for *"wilderness"*. They simply exist, as do the plants and animals with and from which they live. *"Environment"* is the material basis of all life: no indigenous people on earth would ever dream of willfully destroying the wilderness. Their *"nature conservation"* is an organic outgrowth of the oneness of man and nature. For Western conservationists, on the other hand, the *"virgin forest"* is a nostalgic notion; the dream of a paradise lost – Europeans and North Americans have, of course, long since thoroughly annihilated their own primeval forests. A subconscious collective sense of guilt now motivates us to try to save the last remaining *"paradises"* in the Southern Hemisphere, whatever the indigenous people think of the methods. Indigenous peoples and the vast majority of Western conservationists do not speak the same language.

The expulsion of indigenous tribes on the grounds of nature conservancy is a US American invention, introduced in practice for the first time 1851 in Yosemite Valley, in California, when Governor Peter Burnett threatened the local Indians in the valley with a *"war of extinction"*. Major James Savage, who went on to execute the plan, spelled out exactly what the governor's statement meant: *"Satan entered paradise and did all the mischief he could. I intend to be a bigger devil in this Indian paradise than old Satan ever was."*[8]

Some Native Americans managed to survive the asymmetric war. But then naturalist John Muir, founder of The Sierra Club, the world's first nature conservancy society, came along and took care of them, too. Muir knew the Yosemite Valley from his own wilderness wanderings. He, too, expressed revulsion for the indigenous people there. He found them to be *"unclean"*, and was repulsed by their eating habits: a fruit and vegetable diet supplemented with protein from flies and ants. John Muir pressured the federal government in Washington to rid the valley of *"such debased fellow beings"*, and to declare it a US National Park. He maintained the Indians were just *"nomads"* passing through and had never had permanent settlements in the valley. That was an outright falsification of history: for about 4,000 years the Yosemite Valley area had been a cultural homeland and botanical breadbasket of the Miwok, Yokut, Paiute and Ahwahneechee tribes – with fields, meadows, fruits and medicinal herbs.

In 1964 the Wilderness Act was signed into law in the USA giving legal footing to the romantic fiction of a nature paradise untouched by humans. The text of the act defines wilderness as *"... an area where the earth and its community of life are untrampled by man, where man himself is a visitor and does not remain"*. Yosemite National Park has served as a model for the WWF and other major conservationist organizations, such as Conservation International, who have exported the scheme throughout the world. Since the founding of the WWF, the national park ideology has led to mass resettlement in the name of nature conservancy. An estimated 20 million people worldwide have fallen victim to these initiatives. These conservation refugees are without exception people of color: First Nations; black tribes; Adivasi, Pygmy; Dayak and Papua peoples.

Prince Philip Comes Aboard

A final impulse for the establishment of the WWF came from Sir Julian Huxley, evolutionary biologist and president of the British Eugenics Society. In his view *"The expansion of humanity is secondary to the preservation of other species."*[9] Apparently that was especially applicable when the humans poised for *"expansion"* were black. Huxley also held a post at the Royal Institute of International Affairs, a foreign policy think tank that looked at population control, and how the Empire could continue securing natural resources long-term after the loss of its colonies.

In 1960 Huxley headed for Africa to see how the national parks were doing. In some countries the park grounds, with their valuable game stocks, covered more than 20 percent of the nation's total surface area. For three months Huxley travelled through eastern, central, and southern Africa and came to the conclusion that the nascent black governments were ruining the game reserves and national parks. He wrote articles about his observations for The Observer: In Kenya, Tanganyika and Rhodesia the wild animals had all but disappeared, he claimed: *"Throughout the area, cultivation is extending, native cattle are multiplying at the expense of wild animals, poaching is becoming heavier and more organized, ... large areas are being overgrazed and degenerating into semi-deserts, and above and behind all this, the human population is inexorably mounting to press even harder on the limited land space."*[10]

Huxley turned to Max Nicholson for help. The founder of the British organization Nature Conservancy was equally concerned about the developments: *"We felt that under the African governments, all prospect of conservation of nature would be ended."*[11] The two joined forces with respected ornithologist Peter Scott and together came up with the idea of founding a supranational organization that would use powerful financial backing and structural dominance to save the last of the African wilderness paradises that the white man called his own.

On an excursion on the sailing yacht Sceptre in the spring of 1961 Peter Scott asked HRH Prince Philip, Duke of Edinburgh, if he wouldn't like to become president of the new organization. In February 2011, in an interview my colleague Tibet Sinha conducted with Prince Philip at

Buckingham Palace for our film 'The Silence of the Pandas', the Prince couldn't remember if the decisive conversation with Peter Scott had actually taken place on the yacht or on land. He had a vivid recollection, on the other hand, of Peter Scott's leadership proposal, and the fact that he had himself collaborated on the WWF charter. Ah, those happy and glorious early days! His clear, lively eyes sparkled cheerfully. The WWF is Prince Philip's life's work – the only public arena where he can move at his ease, without having to fulfill the role of Prince Consort to the Queen.

Prince Philip summed up the founding story for us in his inimitable laconic upper-crust style: *"Peter Scott said: 'We're going to set this thing up, would I be president?' I said: 'Well, I'll be president of the UK thing, but I won't be president of the international.' Because I happened to be president of the International Equestrian Federation at the time, and I said: 'I can't do two international things at once.' But I said that I happened to know that Prince Bernhard of the Netherlands is very interested in wild animals and conservation, and he happens to be staying at Claridges, so if you pop along and ask him, you may get him, which is what he did."*

Prince Bernhard had, in fact, agreed to take on the presidency, and threw himself wholeheartedly into the task. He and his fellow WWF founders dreamed of creating a contiguous supranational park system stretching from Kenya to South Africa – under their control. On September 11th, 1961, in one of the last convulsions of Empire, the World Wildlife Fund was born, with headquarters in Gland, Switzerland, on the shores of Lake Geneva.

Gerti the Rhinoceros

To get the national parks of Africa whipped into tiptop shape the WWF would need a lot of money – from rich philanthropists and the general public alike. To induce the average working stiff to donate generously, WWF PR tacticians came up with a commercial strategy that the designated Vice President Peter Scott referred to as a *"shock tactic"*. The ad agency Mather & Crowther had apparently searched worldwide for horrifying images of animal massacres. The result was a WWF brochure entitled 'Save the World's Wildlife'.

To effectively spread its message among the common folk, the WWF did a deal with the Daily Mirror, which still had a circulation of over 5 million at the time. On October 9th, 1961 a special issue hit the newsstands: six pages chock-a-block with the most gruesome pictures from the WWF brochure. The front page sported a photo of mama Rhinoceros Gerti side-by-side with her baby, along with a dramatic appeal to the conscience of readers: *"DOOMED to disappear from the face of the earth … UNLESS something is done swiftly, animals like this rhino and its baby will soon be as dead as the dodo."* The ill-fated dodo bird, that iconic poster child of extinction, was an effective reference for stirring public sympathies.

The shock treatment had encouraging results: within four days 20,000 people had donated money to the WWF to help save the endangered animals – in the belief that their hard-earned savings would actually go to help Gerti and her kind. But according to the research of British journalist Kevin Dowling the WWF did not invest a single penny of the proceeds from this first big fundraising campaign in saving the endangered rhinos. Not until twelve years later, it seems, did WWF funds finally make their way into an initiative to help save the rhinoceros.[12] I wanted to dig deeper, so I contacted WWF South Africa, but they refused my request for an interview.

Apparently the WWF had no guilty conscience about manipulating the good will of the donors. On the contrary, it took unscrupulous advantage of people's sympathy with the plight of the animals. Clear evidence of this can be found in a lecture given by WWF co-founder Max Nicholson shortly after the first big donation drive at an event with WWF campaign managers in Zurich. Nicholson blithely enthused: *"We have, therefore, good confirmation of our diagnosis of the publicity value of the world wildlife emergency and the possibilities of converting it into effective money-raising."*[13]

The ploy was so effective that the WWF has continued to use it, more or less unaltered, to this day. The focus shifts every year to a different protagonist from a roster of *"charismatic"* animals – tigers, whales, elephants & Co. take turns strumming the heartstrings of the public.

Oil in Their Blood

In 1962, when Prince Bernhard of the Netherlands took office as President of WWF International, he brought an old friend on board as a major sponsor: John H. Loudon, General Director of petrochemicals giant Royal Dutch Shell. That was a bonanza for the WWF, but was also the source of much friction with other nature conservancy organizations – at the time, Shell was generating its biggest profits with patents on pesticides based on chlorinated hydrocarbons.[14]

In that same year of 1962 several scientific journals revealed that these very pesticides were extremely hazardous for wild animals. There had been repeated mass die-offs of birds that had pecked at grain and seeds treated with Shell products. Instead of a serious self-critical response to the findings, the company responded with a salvo of counter-studies from subservient scientists.

In its effort to fend off the unpleasant truth Shell could rely completely on the help of the WWF. Prince Bernhard himself distributed an argument paper from Shell boss John H. Loudon to the WWF Board of Trustees. In his paper, Loudon asked the WWF to refrain from expressing criticism about the hazardous substances. He emphasized the *"humanitarian usefulness"* of the pesticides, which lay in their ability to prevent famine in the world.[15]

Sir Peter Scott, the renowned British bird lover, was the only one at the meeting of WWF leadership elite to raise a voice of dissent against the audacious argumentation advanced by Shell. Sir Peter said that, in truth, *"greed"* and the *"total disregard of the natural environment"* posed the largest threat to life on earth. But he, too, failed in the end to insist on a public condemnation of WWF sponsor Shell. It was agreed that a decision on the matter be postponed – in fact, the WWF remained silent on the subject in the years that followed. The silence lasted until the mid-1970s, when the subject of CHC pesticides conveniently took care of itself: they were finally banned in the USA and most other countries on earth.

Over the years there were repeated debates in the WWF Executive Committee about whether they should be accepting financial contributions form *"irresponsible"* businesses. After protracted consideration, in the early 1980s the committee finally arrived at the definitive decision: better not to be so strict. It was *"difficult to impossible"* to make a moral judgment about a company. According to the minutes of an Executive Committee meeting, one member even quoted the Church as a precedent: *"It was observed that no church refused donations from sinners."*[16]

Three years after the pesticide scandal the relationship with the oil multinational had grown even closer. In 1966 John H. Loudon, by that time no longer General Director of Shell but Chairman of its Supervisory Board, became a member of the Executive Committee of WWF International, on the recommendation of Prince Bernhard. The oil industry could now have an even more direct influence on the environmental strategy of the biggest nature conservancy organization on Earth. That would pay off just a year later.

On March 18th, 1967 the oil tanker Torrey Canyon ran aground on a reef in the English Channel. The supertanker, which was chartered by British Petroleum (BP), broke apart; 200 kilometers of British and French coastal areas were contaminated by a massive oil spill – the first in post-war history. 15,000 seabirds died an agonizing death, and the oil industry came under massive public fire. The WWF alone showed polite restraint. The International Executive Committee decided not to join other environmental groups in their condemnation of BP and others *"as this might compromise further fund-raising efforts and approaches to certain industries, particularly in the United States."*[17] The WWF top brass made only one concession, allowing the British section to launch a *"seabird appeal"*, which went on to raise 5,000 pounds sterling. The money was used to support the de-oiling and resettlement of the birds. The WWF contented itself with cleaning up the mess made by its industrial partner. A business model with a future?

Old Pals

In 1975 a US Senate sub-committee led by Senator Frank Church was convened to investigate alleged illegal payments by the arms manufacturer Lockheed. The hearings revealed that the US firm had also arranged for bribery payments to Prince Bernhard, in exchange for orders by the Netherlands for Lockheed's Orion fighter jets. In its own investigation report from August 1976 the Dutch government acknowledged that the corruption charges had been founded.

Denial would have been folly anyway, as Prince Bernhard had left an all too obvious trail of evidence behind – including a handwritten letter to the arms company in which the Prince petitioned them for two million dollars commission. Too much, said the Lockheed bosses and sent manager Roger Bixby Smith to the Netherlands. At a meeting with the Prince at Soestdijk Palace they agreed on a compromise: Lockheed would transfer one million dollars for Bernhard to a numbered account in Geneva, on the condition that the Dutch government ordered at least four Orion jets. When the story eventually came to light, Prince Bernhard said in his defense that the money had all been for a good cause – the WWF. However, he was never able to prove this.

In 1995, while researching the history of the WWF, British journalist Kevin Dowling discovered that Prince Bernhard had acted as a lobbyist for the US Lockheed concern since 1959 – long before the bribery scandal. Dr. Max Ilgner, an old friend from the Nazi era, had brokered the contact. The former management board member of the notorious IG Farben chemical company had done his time for war crimes, and was now working for Lockheed. At IG Farben Max Ilgner had headed the NW7 department (industrial espionage), among other things. One of his subordinates had been Prince Bernhard zur Lippe-Biesterfeld, who worked as an assistant manager at the Paris branch.[18]

In 1937 the Prince left the company to marry the Dutch crown princess Juliane. Prince Bernhard hadn't just been an IG Farben spy, but a member of the elite Nazi cavalry regiment, the Reiter-SS, as well – a biographical detail that he prudently withheld from the Dutch.

When the Lockheed scandal broke in 1976 Prince Bernhard became untenable as President of the WWF and, at the request of the Executive Committee, resigned the office. His friend John H. Loudon, Chairmen of the Board of Dutch Royal Shell, followed the Prince into the post. Contrary to the fears of WWF headquarters, the Lockheed scandal in the Netherlands led to only a minor dip in donations to the WWF. It takes more than a bit of corporate corruption to shake the faith of a true Panda believer.

Prince Bernhard left a political legacy that in some ways still influences the style and internal culture of the WWF today. The Prince, for example, had a soft spot for secret societies: he founded not only the elite, and for a long time top secret, Bilderberg Group, but also the sub-rosa WWF *"order"* known as The 1001 Club. The Prince also introduced the exclusive honors system that continues to contribute to the elite self-image of the contemporary organization.

The highest WWF honor is The Order of the Golden Ark, awarded *"in recognition of special service to the conservation of the world's flora and fauna."* If someone who hasn't actually performed the special service is nevertheless dying to wear the medal to the next Panda Ball, a donation of at least 100,000 dollars will do. Several rich aesthetes, such as Laurance Spelman Rockefeller, have elected for this option to get the hardware.

The second category in the WWF honors ranking, the Gold Medal for Outstanding Contemporary Conservationists, is less expensive. The WWF didn't even have to pay for the gold the medal is made of – the South African Chamber of Commerce donated it. Honorees in this category also get a gold Rolex watch for their troubles.

One of the first recipients of the gold medal plus Rolex was Prof. Dr. Bernhard Grzimek, also a member of The 1001 Club. The Director of the Frankfurt Zoo embodied like no other the romantic soul of the WWF. Month for month, his raspy philanthropist's voice invoked the call of the wild from TV sets and in movie theatres. Despite his key role as poster boy for the WWF, Grzimek was an exotic specimen in The 1001 Club; almost all the other members were wealthy businesspeople who responded more to the call of cash than to that of the wilderness. These global players, such as Paris born, Swiss schooled British citizen and resident of Switzerland, the billionaire and hereditary religious leader Prince Sadruddin Aga Khan, knew how to harmoniously combine nature conservancy and business. The Aga Khan, too, was a member of the secret WWF club and also served as Vice President of WWF International. His mighty and ancient family clan had invested billions in African countries – which certainly did no harm to the power base and informal political network of the WWF.

The 250 square kilometre floor of the Ngorongoro crater in Tanzania is home to thousands of elephants, buffalo, rhinoceros, flamingos and lions: the crater is a veritable Garden of Eden and is known as the *"eighth wonder of the world"*. The Massai were allowed to resettle there after being kicked out of the Serengeti. The crater offered salt and water for the Massai cattle. Then, two years after the mass resettlement, Tanganyika became independent.

In the new state of Tanzania that was formed after unification with Zanzibar, the white WWF functionaries held powerful sway. They controlled the national parks, and thus the flow of money to Africa for the protection of the national parks from the international nature conservancy organizations and Western countries. The conservationist lobby put persistent pressure on the government of the young country to have the Massai expelled from the new settlement area as well: the Ngorongoro nature reserve was overgrazed, and the Massai used too much water. The nature conservationists achieved their aim; in 1974 the Massai were forced to clear off once again.

The government sent military troops into the Ngorongoro who proceeded to drive the people from their huts and burn them down while the inhabitants looked on.[19] The soldiers also opened the kraals – the traditional livestock enclosures that form the centerpiece of a village – and drove the herds out of the crater. When the cattle instinctively returned, they were shot dead. Massai who resisted were bludgeoned and thrown into jail.

As soon as the mud huts of the Massai were gone, the tourism business took over, erecting huge tent campsites where thousands of tourists were allowed to stay. Promoters such as The Sierra Club offered *"campers"* from Europe and the USA luxury tents with real feather beds, hot showers and ice-cold beer. The ice was produced using generators that made an almighty racket in the crater day and night, and there was no longer any mention of water shortages.

In 1992 the government finally managed to enact a prohibition against camping in the crater basin. It was a triumph for the Ngorongoro Nature Reserve, but it would soon prove to be a Pyrrhic victory: not long afterwards a powerful investor appeared with plans for a luxury hotel smack in the middle of the conservation area, right on the edge of the crater. The park administration vetoed the proposal but the president of the country overruled them, ordering them to issue a special permit for the project. The investor wasn't just anyone, after all, but a special *"friend"* of the nation: the Ismaili Muslim hereditary Imam and multibillionaire HRH Prince Karim Aga Khan IV, member of the WWF 1001 Club and nephew of WWF Vice President Prince Sadruddin Aga Khan.

The nature reserve authorities were forced to bow to their higher-ups. An ecological disaster was predictable, because after the grand opening celebrations for the Serena Safari Lodge in 1996 safari tourism kicked in big time. For 630 dollars a night in the peak season tourists can now reside in a luxury hotel with all the creature comforts, right in the middle of the wilderness. Since then, 150 jeeps a day have rumbled through the crater – for a big game photo shoot. After the thrills of the safari there is afternoon tea at the crater's edge with live entertainment: Massai warriors in their traditional red capes perform tribal dances for the upscale ecotourists, and the hotel offers excursions to *"traditional Massai villages"*. The noble herdsmen have become dancing beggars, living from the alms of the tourist industry.

The Aga Khan's hotel and the neighboring hotel Ngorongoro Sopa, which was built later, consume an enormous amount of water. To serve their needs they pump fresh water out of the crater, and as a result more and more salt water from the Ngorongoro salt lake has seeped into the ground water. The forests in the crater are now dying as a consequence of salinization. But the tourists needn't feel troubled because, once again, the blame for the crisis is being placed squarely on the shoulders of the Massai, although they are only allowed to enter the crater once a day to give their cattle salt and water. A third resettlement of the Massai is already under discussion. On the edge of the crater not far from the Aga Khan's hotel a pyramid of unpolished stones rises up, marking a burial site. Here lies the mortal remains of Prof. Bernhard Grzimek and his son Michael. The Serengeti crusaders are gone, but their spirit lives on.

Skeletons in the Cupboard

Any unauthorized individual who penetrates the inner sanctum of the WWF pays dearly for it, as did British journalist Kevin Dowling. In 1990 Dowling, who had first made his name with nature films, came into the possession of internal WWF documents, including the 1001 Club membership list. And he would pay a heavy price indeed. His film 'The Secret of the Rhinoceros' about the secret African life of the WWF, was never shown; the research results disappeared into the archives of English TV broadcaster Channel 4. Dowling's career was in tatters: *"I didn't stand a chance, because the WWF has connections that are just too powerful."* Dowling never regained a professional foothold, earning his living with articles for a provincial newspaper until he died, an ailing and bitter man, in 2008. But he had been too good a journalist to just consign his discoveries to obscurity. He had made copies of secret documents and taken precautions to ensure that, one day, they would reemerge.

I picked up Kevin Dowling's trail on the Internet. A report in the Dutch newspaper 'Algemeen Dagblad' from January 17th, 2000 caught my eye: a Dutch lawyer called

J. G. G. Wilgers had won a court case against the WWF, enabling him to use the term *"criminal organization"* to describe the WWF without fear of further legal repercussions. I called the lawyer in Goes, the Netherlands. He was immediately on fire, and very forthcoming: *"In the early days, the WWF used the cover of nature conservancy to engage in criminal activities. Did you know that a commando with WWF connections allegedly even murdered people opposing the apartheid regime in South Africa?"* For a moment I seriously considered just hanging up – the honorable attorney from Goes obviously had an overactive imagination. On the other hand: if his accusations were false, why had he been acquitted? I asked if he would be willing to repeat his assertions in a recorded interview and to provide evidence to back them up. Wilgers hesitated before answering: *"I would certainly be willing, but there's someone who knows more than I do."* That someone was René Zwaap, who lives in the center of Amsterdam near the train station. I met him as arranged at a bustling and drafty Chinese restaurant called Yan.

René Zwaap was a thin, slightly bent man in his mid-forties with a big bushy head of hair and wire-rimmed glasses. He greeted all the Chinese waiters present by name. Before the Peking duck had landed on our table he had already smoked three cigarettes and run me through his biography: he was currently editor of the online news site Public Affairs; before that he wrote for the hard-hitting Dutch news weekly 'De Groene Amsterdammer'; he was busy at the moment working on two documentary films about the military history of the Netherlands and on a book about Prince Bernhard.

The German prince at the side of the popular Dutch monarch Queen Juliane had really turned Zwaap's head: *"Bernhard has had a greater influence on Dutch history than people think. I once researched his time at IG Farben for a Dutch newspaper. Prince Bernhard got wind of it and summoned my publisher in to see him. They had a chat and ended up becoming good pals. Later my boss showed me a postcard he had received from Prince Bernhard. On the back was written: why is that impudent guy still working for you?"*

René Zwaap had stumbled upon the inglorious interlude in the prince's career by chance: *"In 1997 I went to England to visit the journalist Kevin Dowling; someone had told me he had a copy of Prince Bernhard's Reiter-SS ID card. And he did actually have it. He gave it to me, asking nothing in return. But he did have something he wanted to get off his chest. I immediately sensed that it was something very important, so I recorded our conversation on film, with an Hi8 camera."*

The faded, pixilated video material shows images of Kevin Dowling as the epitome of the slightly down-at-heel conservative British gentleman: in a grey pinstriped suit with a red and brown striped tie he sits in a wing-back chair in the midst of a landscape of bookshelves, porcelain figurines, little rubber trees and other bric-a-brac. He speaks – five hours long – of his battle with the WWF, which ended for him in a complete and crushing defeat. The video is the legacy of a failed hero.

In 1989 he shot his first documentary film charting the fate of the big game animals. It was called 'The Elephant Man', and revealed that poachers in Africa had slaughtered a million elephants. The viewing public was deeply

Kevin Dowling, 1997

unsettled and donations flooded in to the WWF – in record amounts. *"I had the numbers about the slaughtered elephants from the WWF,"* said Kevin Dowling. *"I had already started to have my doubts while shooting the film, because where would the Africans in Kenya, Zambia, and Tanzania get enough weapons to kill a million elephants? Before the film was finished I knew: the number was incorrect. The WWF must have known better. I believe it **is** possible that they fed me the false number to sway public opinion towards taking tougher measures against game poachers. I completed the film nevertheless, and the WWF even gave me an award for it. But my doubts weighed heavily."*

Kevin Dowling headed out to Africa once more, but this time his aim was to uncover the secrets of the WWF. In 1992, British broadcaster ITV aired the results of Dowling's research in a TV documentary titled: 'Ten Pence in the Panda'. The film was one of the first critical explorations of the colonial antecedents of the WWF. It was aired only once, before disappearing into the station's archives. I tried to get at least a preview copy from ITV – in vain. Even 20 years after its single airing, the documentary remains under lockdown. I kept looking, but the search seemed jinxed: I tired all the relevant libraries and film archives, but no one had a copy. The political and media allies of the WWF had apparently done a good clean-up job – after all, Dowling's findings amounted to a powder keg of negative PR for the WWF. Among other things, he believed he had found solid evidence of misappropriation of donation funds. In front of René's camera Kevin Dowling takes a ring binder from a bookcase and opens it. He claims it contains secret internal WWF documentation: The Phillipson Report.

In 1987 the WWF commissioned Oxford economist John Phillipson to do a comprehensive company audit. WWF management was probably less-than-thrilled with the prospect, but the investigation was being done at the express wish of South African tobacco tycoon Anton Rupert. He had been able to demand such a thing because, according to Dowling, he was paying the salary of the WWF General Director out of his own pocket. This too, remained a heavily guarded WWF secret for many years. Rupert wanted to know how efficient the international projects of the WWF actually were, and how management could be improved.

The result of the audit was unambiguous: the WWF produced *"few"* long-term successes, and the organization was accused of *"egocentricity and neo-colonialism"* in the developing world where WWF practice discriminated against local staff: *"They resent not being consulted about or informed of the conservation initiatives in their own countries."* The report called the financial conduct of the WWF *"appalling"*. Only the pressure applied by Prince Philip himself, who by that time was already President of WWF International, could persuade inspector Phillipson to soften his assessment to: *"leaves much to be desired"*. But Phillipson's verdict on project accounting, and thus the allocation of donation monies, remained damning: *"a diligent auditor set among the project account files in Switzerland would surely open a cupboard full of skeletons."* The auditor could find no documentation at all for many field projects; for others there was no record of the specific allocation of funds.

Prince Philip wrote an outraged letter to WWF General Director Charles de Haes: *"I had no idea that it might land us in such a pickle!! Whatever we do with it, we are bound to get into trouble. If we don't publish it in full, we are bound to be accused of trying to 'cover up' something. If we do let it out, all the mischief-makers will have field day!"*[20]

The prince advised against distributing the highly explosive report to the WWF Executive Committee. Of the 208 pages of the audit, a grand total of 9 were distributed in the end. Prince Philip had rightly feared a slump in donations should the findings of the auditor be made public – some of them were the stuff of a public image meltdown. For example, Phillipson assessed the WWF campaign to save the panda as follows: *"The WWF made no serious attempt to successfully implement its panda pro-*

gram ... donors would be dismayed to discover that their capital contribution is basically a complete write-off."

Kevin Dowling's film 'Ten Pence in the Panda' put a few big dents in the WWF image, but the public debate soon ebbed away. But Dowling was not prepared to cease and desist – he still had ammunition in reserve. The commissioning editors at public service broadcaster Channel 4 were thrilled when Dowling pitched them his new film project.

Operation Lock

During the course of his investigation Dowling had come upon information about Operation Lock, a military commando in which the WWF had had a hand. In 1987 the WWF had contracted British private security company KAS to deploy a mercenary unit to combat the black market trade in ivory and rhinoceros horn.

In 1996 the South African government under Nelson Mandela appointed a commission to investigate criminal activities carried out by the apartheid regime under the cover of nature conservancy. Judge Mark Kumleben, who led the investigation committee, discovered that the former South African government had secretly organized mass slaughter of elephant and rhinoceros stocks in neighboring Black-governed countries, primarily Angola.

The main goal of the secret service operation was to politically and economically destabilize neighboring countries with Black governments, in an effort to undermine their public credibility. *"You see,"* the message would be, *"the Blacks just can't manage on their own."* South Africa's Kruger National Park looked all the better in contrast: the WWF praised it to the rafters worldwide, and funneled donation money into it. Eyewitnesses testified before judge Kumleben that warehouses belonging to the South African military secret service had been used for the illegal transit of 3,000 pairs of poached elephant tusks a month.

Judge Kumleben also looked into the existence of the secret WWF commando unit, though apparently not very deeply. The judge heard witness Mike Richards, an agent of the South African secret police. He had been an undercover plant in the WWF mercenary group, meant to keep it under control – and to gather information. He testified that Operation Lock had been *"advantageous"* because *"the network needed for the collection and collation of information concerning endangered species and wild-life products takes on the same format as an infrastructure which is needed for the collection and collation of intelligence directly related to the activities of anti-South African countries, forces and people."*[21]

Dowling's research started where Kumleben's investigations had left off. He was certain that: *"Only portions of the Kumleben Report had been published. Mandela didn't want it made public that the WWF was aware of the dirty dealings of the apartheid regime. He didn't want to make waves with Great Britain; he also liked the Dutch Prince Bernhard and saw him as a friend."*[22]

Several newspapers confirmed Kevin Dowling's claim: that the WWF special unit was aware of the animal slaughter orchestrated by the South African secret service. Colonel Ian Crooke, commander of the KAS, even signed a contract swearing himself and all his men to secrecy regarding South Africa's involvement in game poaching and ivory smuggling. In return for their silence the office of the president issued the mercenaries false documents and passports, which gave them freedom of movement. Craig Williamson, a top South African secret service agent, testified before Dowling's camera that he had personally handed the false papers over to Colonel Crooke, commander of the secret unit that had been active since November 1987 in South Africa and its neighboring countries. The KAS team had been headquartered at a safe house, first in Pretoria, later in Johannesburg.

Kevin Dowling's assertions were by no means plucked from thin air; other sources back them up. I went to meet Prof. Stephen Ellis at the African Studies Centre in Leiden, the Netherlands. At the time of the events in question he had edited the London-based military, political and social analysis newsletter 'Africa Confidential'. Back in 1990, an insider had passed internal WWF documents to him: *"I don't want to name the source, but at no time did the WWF ever contest the authenticity of the documents. Their contents make clear that Prince Bernhard had hatched the idea, together with South African WWF functionary John Hanks. At the time, Hanks was the WWF chief in charge of Africa. The two of them hired a private security company made up of former soldiers from the elite British SAS unit. They appeared in South Africa, contracted to track down and eliminate black-marketeers of rhinoceros. The WWF tried to play down its complicity in the activities by emphasizing that Prince Bernhard was no longer president of WWF International at the time, but of the Dutch WWF organization only. The WWF secretariat in Gland, Switzerland had known nothing about any of it. Bernhard and John Hanks did, in fact, end up taking full responsibility, in order to exonerate WWF International. But the truth is, the leadership of WWF International was involved in the planning as well."*

There is a solid piece of evidence to support Stephen Ellis' allegation: a letter from then-General Secretary of WWF South Africa Frans Stroebel to Prince Philip, still president of WWF International at the time. Stroebel had personally introduced the commanders of Operation Lock to the officers of the South African secret service, and had participated from day one in planning the paramilitary activities. In his January 1990 letter to Prince Philip, Stroebel reveals that he had briefed WWF International General secretary Charles de Haes on Operation Lock from the very beginning – in other words, from the fall of 1987 at the latest: *"I have given Mr. de Haes a number of comprehensive briefings on the project since I first became involved. In May 1989, I gave him full details. He then went to HRH Prince Bernhard to confirm that Prince Bernhard was indeed the sponsor. Mr. de Haes satisfied himself with the developments, and in subsequent discussions with me he never expressed any concern about my involvement, or, for that matter, the covert programme itself."*[23] According to Dowling's findings, Prince Bernhard hired the company in 1987 and paid for its services in a rather unusual manner: He took two valuable Old Master paintings from the royal art collection of his wife, Queen Juliane of the Netherlands, and had them auctioned at Sotheby's. The Murillo picture 'The Holy

Family' did most to fill the war chest, selling at almost a million dollars. Prince Bernhard donated the profits to WWF International. Then the WWF pulled something out of its bag of tricks to obscure the money trail. Prof. Stephen Ellis explained: *"I later found out that the WWF transferred the money back to Prince Bernhard in a secret transaction. He then used it to pay the KAS security company's commando unit."*[24] Armed with this knowledge, Kevin Dowling and his team had gone to Africa to find out more about the mercenary unit, which had consisted, for the most part, of former officers of the elite British special forces unit Special Air Service, or SAS. Its legendary founder Sir David Sterling had gone on to found the private security company KAS Enterprises. Like Prince Bernhard he, too, had donated money to finance the undercover operation in South Africa.

Kevin Dowling was still researching for the film when pressure on the TV station began to mount. One day the head of Channel 4 called Dowling into his office: *"He said to me 'of course we'll continue working on this project, but lawyers from the WWF have informed us that you're biased on this subject. It would be better if someone else took over as director.'"* To save the film, Dowling agreed – from then on, he was officially just a *"consultant"* on his own film project. The important thing was to keep going and get the job done, because his investigation was leading him down new and ever deeper rabbit holes.

Former South African secret service operatives testified for Dowling on camera that the mercenaries deployed by the WWF weren't only interested in game poachers. Their commander offered support to the South

African secret service in its fight against the African National Congress, or ANC, anti-apartheid movement. The original South African witness statements were locked up in some archive somewhere but, in his filmed testimony for René Zwaap, Kevin Dowling was able to draw on the transcriptions he had made of the interviews at the time: *"The KAS mercenaries used the Kruger National Park as a training grounds to train paramilitary units such as the Koevoet Squad from Namibia. They were then deployed against the ANC as part of the so-called 'third force'. This officially non-existent execution squad murdered around 6,000 opponents of the apartheid regime in South Africa."*

It remains unclear whether WWF top brass knew of the war crimes committed by KAS mercenaries under the pretext of nature conservancy. Dowling could only presume so: *"After all, high-ranking WWF functionaries were among the management of Kruger National Park. The special units were trained in the park, and there was also a secret prison for apartheid opponents on park grounds."* – a serious allegation that I wanted to query John Hanks about. He's still one of the leading nature conservationists in South Africa. He answered my request, writing to say that he would be prepared to give an interview about the history of the WWF in South Africa. An appointment for the interview was confirmed, but then he called it off: he had *"heard"* that I wanted to ask him about Operation Lock. In his written withdrawal Hanks said: *"I'm not prepared to talk about Operation Lock. Please remove the interview from your schedule."*

Dowling's research revealed that the elite KAS commando unit troops were not only recruited from British

SAS unit veterans. From time to time, active officers from London also appeared in their ranks. For instance, Operation Lock invited a female British army specialist for chemical and biological warfare to come to South Africa for a working visit. It seems Colonel Ian Crooke had come up with a cunning idea: he wanted to saturate the rhino horns with poison. The African smugglers and the consumers of the goods in Asia would die as a result. The aim of this toxic battle tactic was to spread fear and loathing, and to bring the black market trade, and thus the poaching, to an end. There is no evidence that this devious ruse was ever put into practice.

Kevin Dowling continued to investigate and kept turning up new and horrific details of Operation Lock. But it never occurred to him that, slowly but surely, he was becoming a political problem himself. Dowling felt safe, because no one could accuse him of *"ever having been a leftist or radical"*. While he was still putting together the rough cut of the film, it's death knell was rung: *"In several phone calls with the station director, Prince Philip's adjutant made it clear that this film could compromise national security. And that was that."*

For years the WWF had obscured and glossed over Operation Lock. Finally, in 2011, WWF leadership allowed Swiss historian Alexis Schwarzenbach access to the archives. He authored the official history of the WWF, published on the occasion of the 50th anniversary of the organization. In the chapter entitled 'Operation Lock' Schwarzenbach admits that, according to internal letters and documents, not only had South African WWF functionaries and Prince Bernhard been involved in the undercover operation, so too had WWF International. WWF President Prince Philip had also been briefed in early 1989.

Historian Schwarzenbach also deserves praise for breaking with the years-long practice of denial and suppression on a further point: he concedes in the book that Operation Lock was about more than just hunting down poachers. Ian Crooke, commander of the WWF special unit, had cooperated with the South African army in their fight against the liberation movement: *"He also offered his services to the South African Defense Force in their struggle against the ANC and other opponents of the apartheid regime."*[25]

But the WWF's soul-searching came too late for Kevin Dowling. His explosive interviews disappeared into the Channel 4 toxic materials vault. It's about time the station finally released the documentation, because despite the piecemeal, partial confessions of the WWF, many questions still remain unanswered. Significant among them: how deeply were the WWF and KAS, the mercenary commando unit it contracted, actually involved in the South African apartheid regime's brutal war against the ANC and neighboring countries? Crucially, it is still not known whether people were killed as a result of this particular WWF adventure, and if so, how many. In any event, close collaboration with the South African terror regime remains an onerous legacy for the Africa policy of the WWF. Kevin Dowling's attempts to pitch his material to Fleet Street fell on deaf ears: the newspapers had no appetite for publishing the controversial story. And Kevin Dowling didn't have the strength to abandon it. *"He was obsessed with the story,"* his friend René Zwaap remembered – *"in the end it killed him."*

The Purge of the Batwa

WWF staff are now more frequently prepared to admit that there *"used to be"* problems in Africa, but they assert that the WWF has learned from its mistakes. In 2000 the first internal criticism of Operation Lock was voiced: the new General Director Claude Martin described the adventure as an example of an *"imperialistic attitude"*. He saw to it that the WWF established national offices in the countries of Asia, Africa and Latin America to help the organization shed the last vestiges of its neocolonial pedigree. In addition, Chris Weaver, the head of WWF Namibia, devised the *"conservancies"* system, which would see entire village communities integrated into the work of the nature reserves, with a share in the proceeds from ecotourism.

The WWF is proud of such tentative attempts at self-reform, but have they really enabled the organization to overcome its colonial heritage? I came across a report to the United Nations expert group on the Rights of Indigenous People. The subject was the fate of the Batwa Pygmy tribe, which, in 1991, had been expelled from its homeland within a national park in southern Uganda.

The report from July 2011 detailed the situation as follows: *"Like in other cases where national parks have been established under the guidance of the WWF and other external forces the indigenous population that had lived there for hundreds or thousands of years in a sustainable way has been evicted from their forest ... Their forests have been given into the hands of foreign investors. Tourism is big business, as the fees for hunting go up to the thousands, or even tens of thousands of dollars for the killing of a single animal, depending on the game species. Under the cloak of conservationism, the investors want 'their' forests for their purposes alone, without any Pygmies."*[26]

I travelled to Berlin to meet Dr. Arnold Groh, the man who had written the high-octane report. He heads a research institute at the Technische Universität (TU) Berlin devoted to the structural analysis of cultural systems. Dr. Groh is a slim, elegantly dressed man with delicate hands and sensitive facial features. His Spartan office was decorated with a huge blow-up of a photo of himself, dressed only in shorts, surrounded by members of the Batwa tribe: *"When we go to visit them, we adapt to their ways, in manner of dress, too – it's a matter of respect. Because everything we introduce there from our industrialized culture changes the norms, and sends a visual message: see, I'm wearing a safari suit, so I'm something better."* He described the ecotourism kick-started by the WWF as insensitive: it stormed into the Pygmy villages like an *"invasion"*, destroying the cultural identity of the tribes.

The WWF, said Dr. Groh, had a *"fundamental"* problem with indigenous peoples: *"Institutions such as the WWF are at least partly responsible for the eradication of indigenous cultures, because very often a forced eviction on the grounds of 'nature conservancy' is the preface to their demise. Without their forest, in which they have lived for millennia, they are exposed to the attacks of other ethnic groups, who hold them in disdain. I observed the fate of the Batwa from close quarters. After they lost their forest, the members of the tribe fell into a deep depression. They started to get drunk in the afternoon, or take drugs – the desperation was palpable in all the villages that I visited."*

To prevent famine in the Batwa tribes the Ugandan government finally granted them permission to hunt again – on the peripheries of their former forest home. They are now allowed to go two kilometers into the rainforest, but no more: the core zone is reserved for mountain gorillas and tourists. The WWF had conducted studies showing that the Batwa could be retrained as farmers. The idea was divorced from reality: there was no agricultural land left for the Batwa to farm.

Just to survive the Batwa now have to work on farms belonging to Bantu, a majority ethnicity in Uganda. Many Bantu see the Batwa as second-class citizens and pay them starvation wages. Some Batwa women resort to prostitution in exchange for food; in Dr. Groh's experience most of the women are simply raped by Bantu: *"I estimated that about 80 percent of Batwa women have been raped. You can see the result in the villages: many of the youth are two heads taller than their mothers; they are half-castes who don't know where they belong. So this ethnicity will soon be genetically extinct as well."*

WWF websites paint a more idyllic picture of the Batwa's situation. One text, in finest colonial prose, reads: *"In 1991, when Uganda's Bwindi Impenetrable National Park (BINP) was declared, to protect endangered mountain gorillas, the community of Mukona Parish protested by setting fire to around 10 sq km of forest. In 1998 the same villagers walked five hours, without any remuneration or incentive,*

Dr. Arnold Groh with the Baygeli, Uganda

to put out a fire that had started accidentally, according to a WWF case study."[27]

Thanks to the positive educational influence of the WWF the bad savages had become good savages – isn't that the message written between the lines? What the reader is not told is that the Pygmies had only set fire to the forest in 1991 because they had been evicted from their huts with military force. The WWF text follows this historical misrepresentation with a passage that heaps praise upon itself: a WWF field study had concluded that the Batwa Pygmies had *"profited"* from the transformation of their land into a human-free national park as they had *"been able to diversify their sources of income"*; tourism in particular had offered many new opportunities:

"They benefit from park and tourism-related employment and from tourism-related revenue ... Training and other opportunities have advanced the organizing, negotiating and business skills of communities."[28]

UN expert Arnold Groh rates this description of conditions as *"hypocrisy, used to justify serious human rights violations after the fact"*. After the expulsion of the Batwa and other indigenous peoples, European and American companies had been granted permission to market the Ugandan national park. Tourism is the most profitable business sector there. In Dr. Groh's opinion, the tour operators see the Batwa *"not as people but as objects"*, which promise additional revenues: *"The tourists are carted into the Batwa villages in safari suits to ogle the naked savages, who have to perform tribal dances for them in a hall financed by the European Union. It's an ethnological zoo that is deeply degrading for the ethnicities in question."*

In their dealings with the Pygmies, said Dr. Groh, WWF functionaries often behaved like members of a *"master race"*, who took the liberty of bringing unsolicited *"progress"* to the *"primitives"*: clothing, running water, houses made of concrete. *"In reality, this strategy leads to the extinction of indigenous cultures. I've often asked myself: why are we making such a desperate effort to extinguish the memory of our natural life as thoroughly as possible? Indigenous peoples don't need the goods of industrialized cultures; nor do they need money or market relationships. All of these products of our dominant culture destroy the cultural self-confidence of the tribes."*

Once a year a few individual Batwa, selected by the authorities, are allowed back into the forest – for one day, under supervision – to gather medicinal plants. It is the one really happy day of the year for the Batwa. They can expect no help from the WWF – the organization itself profits directly from their expulsion. WWF USA, for example, organizes a tour through the Ugandan national parks that it bills as: The Great African Primate Expedition. The highlight of the 11,000-dollar adventure – air travel to Uganda not included – is *"Gorilla trekking"*. The WWF hawks the tour by highlighting the guaranteed Batwa-free jungle route: *"No other encounter in the wilderness can surpass the thrill of meeting up with one of these wonderful animals that are so similar to us."*

For Dr. Arnold Groh it was an open-and-shut case: *"It's not about protecting the animals, it's about using them to do business. If the WWF really wanted to conserve nature, they would have to ensure that the Batwa are able to return to their forests. For thousands of years they have maintained the balance among species."*

The Batwa, he explained, had never posed a threat to the gorilla population. Nor had they ever threatened the stocks of elephants or other animals native to Uganda's rainforest: *"They only took from the forest and its game stocks what they needed to live. Since the eviction of the Batwa, big game hunters have been wreaking havoc in the national parks in the name of 'regulating' animal stocks. It's a very lucrative business for the hunting industry, but also for the government. It makes a lot of money on elephant-hunting permits."*

In the catalogue of a European hunting tour operator I actually found an ad with a detailed offer: A permit to shoot a Ugandan elephant for a fee of 36,000 euros – for this price the marksman even gets to take the ivory of its *"prey"* back home.

The Return of the White Hunters

After my meeting with Dr. Arnold Groh in Berlin I was walking past the Tiergarten commuter rail station when I noticed a huge WWF campaign billboard. It pictured a mother elephant with one front leg planted protectively in front of her young. The headline above the picture: *"Born to Live. 5 Euros Will Give Him a Habitat in Africa."* Reading the small print, donors would have discovered that their money was destined for the new Kavango–Zambezi Transfrontier Conservation Area (KAZA).

KAZA: a project that would see a collection of 36 national parks and reserves in Zimbabwe, Angola, Botswana, Zambia and Namibia joined together in a giant contiguous network. The WWF currently invests 2.7 million dollars a year in this ambitious project that, if the WWF website is to be believed, will save the elephants of Africa: *"They're in a tight squeeze … support the WWF rescue operations – they're the only chance the elephants have of survival."* In a promotional video the WWF promotes KAZA as a means of *"fighting poverty"*, because the residents of the area would have a share in the proceeds from the *"sustainable use of animals and plants"*.

The WWF propaganda prudently fails to tell potential donors what *"use of animals"* might refer to. Studying the KAZA website I found an altogether different version of the heart-rending elephant story. According to their telling, the elephant population wasn't too small, thus in need of protection. On the contrary, apparently it was too big. The main problem faced by the nations involved was how to reduce elephant numbers: there were 250,000 of them living in the *"transfrontier"* park area – double the desired number. In their search for food the elephants were threatening the vegetation and destroying farmer's fields.

Nearly all KAZA-project participant nations were planning to introduce elephant hunting as an industry. The KAZA website speaks of elephants as a *"species of superior economic and ecological significance for the region"* and an *"economic asset"*. As the KAZA park's most valuable treasure, the elephants could help to attract investors: *"The reintroduction of legal trade in the products of sustainable stocks of elephants and other animals could be an important basis for investment in this project."*[29]

The WWF prefers not to confront its donors with such profane business straight talk. Instead, it ensnares them in the mawkish yarn of the African elephants that would soon face extinction without the WWF. In truth, WWF partners are currently busy in southern Africa setting up a profitable business with organized big game hunting – of elephants. That can't have escaped the attention of the WWF. To attract elephant hunting punters, the firm Botswana Safaris has a special offer: ca. 13,000 dollars per elephant instead of the usual 45,000+.

I found similar offers for elephant hunting in Zimbabwe's Hwange National Park, which is also part of the Kavango–Zambezi Transfrontier Conservation Area. I am in no position to pass final professional judgment

Angebot für eine Jagd auf Elefant und Leopard und Büffel:	
16 Jagdtage mit Jagdführung 1:1, (Berufsjäger, Fährtenleser, Allradwagen), Unterkunft mit Vollverpflegung im Jagdcamp, täglicher Wäschedienst, Rohpräparation der Trophäen,	
pro Jäger	US$ 39.150,00
+ Trophäengebühr für einen Elefanten(30-53,99lbs)	US$ 15.400,00
+ Trophäengebühr für einen Elefanten(54-63,99lbs)	US$ 18.700,00
+ Trophäengebühr für einen Elefanten(ab 64lbs)	US$ 27.500,00
+ Trophäengebühr für einen Leoparden	US$ 5.445,00

Catalogue offering hunting trips to Africa

on whether or not the elephant hunt makes any ecological sense. However, I do find it clearly immoral that the WWF works both sides of the street, taking advantage of it's donors love of animals with a mendacious campaign aimed at parting them from their money.

It's open season in the KAZA park area, co-conceived and co-financed by the WWF. Shooting permits are available for: lions, elephants, leopards, giraffes, buffalo, crocodiles and rhinoceros. Some British companies even take shooting parties out with bloodhounds to hunt leopard. Africa's big game, its great treasure, is once again in the hands of the white hunters and the Western hunting tour operators: it's almost as happy and glorious as the good old days.

6. Have a Nice Death with the WWF

The WWF is skilled in the art of money-making. For example, the YouTube campaign to solicit funds for the orangutans, our *"jungle cousins"*: to the strains of a melodramatic film score, an orangutan flees the chain saws as they savage the rainforests of Borneo. The orangutan turns his big sad eyes to the viewer. An apocalyptical voiceover intones: *"His home is our climate. Save both. You can help with an SMS. Send 'Borneo' to 81190. WWF – for a living planet."*

It's nice to be able to unburden your heavy conscience in seconds with a simple tap-tap-tap on the smartphone – for a scant 7 dollars. The ploy works, and it doesn't occur to contributors that their insta-donation might not actually go to the orangutans. But what does the WWF really do to help save these great apes? One searches the WWF website in vain for current accounting statements and financial reports with reliable figures. Transparency is not the WWF's strong suit. No one knows exactly where donation monies totaling around 700 million dollars a year end up.

According to the WWF only 8 percent of the total donation funds are used to cover administrative costs; everything else, they claim, goes directly to the projects on site and to support educational work. However, this calculation neglects to itemize the salaries of the organization's full-time staff – these sums are often included in the project expenses and thus concealed. In truth, according to American author Christine MacDonald, personnel costs gobble up nearly 50 percent of the WWF's receipts.[30] The organization has almost 5,000 full-time staff mouths to feed worldwide – and the pay packets of WWF top management are hefty indeed. The CEO of WWF USA alone collects an annual salary of 505,000 dollars.

Borneo Ablaze

Our investigation eventually put us on a plane to Borneo, more precisely to Kalimantan, the Indonesian part of the island. As soon as we landed at Palangkaraya Airport I got an impression of the power the WWF wields in Indonesia. Inside the airport building hung huge posters promoting the Sabangau National Park, which is under the stewardship of the WWF. Instead of the conventional souvenir shop in the main entry hall there was a WWF shop, full of bright brochures telling of the organization's good works in reforestation and the fight against game poachers.

Nordin was waiting for us outside. He heads the human rights organization Save Our Borneo and is a member of the supervisory board of the Indonesian section of Friends of the Earth.

Nordin

He knows every tree trunk in central Kalimantan. The strong, compactly built, always slightly surly man states his profession as *"Activist"*. Nordin is up against powerful opponents, who are rapidly deforesting his homeland to make way for palm oil plantations.

Together with Nordin and his colleague Udin we set out by jeep for the realm of the orangutans. At around midday the thermometer rose to above 40 degrees Celsius. The humidity lay like a dirty film on our skin. The countryside was a lush green: patches of plucked rainforest, between them the fields of forest farmers, and then another brutalized patch, where only the torsos of a few decapitated rainforest giants had been left standing. The lumber companies had arrived twenty 20 years before to mow down the forests.

Only 30 percent of Kalimantan's original rainforest remains. But left in peace, the deforested areas recuperate relatively quickly in the hot, humid local climate. Just a few years on, a secondary forest had already grown up, once again providing a habitat for an astonishingly diverse range of species. Nevertheless, the rainforest is now condemned to certain death: the state has given it as a concession to domestic and foreign palm oil companies. Indonesia's central government has put its chips on the expansion of the palm oil industry, the country's presumed best bet for achieving wealth and power.

The third party in this deal, alongside the Indonesian state and industry, is the WWF. It alone has what it takes to convince the general public in Europe and the USA that intensive palm oil farming can be good not only for the economic development of poor countries like Indonesia and Malaysia, but for the natural environment as well. With the help of the invincible panda, most companies now produce *"sustainable"* palm oil, for which allegedly only *"degraded"* forests are cleared, and not the *"virgin"* rainforests of Asia and the Americas.

Nordin had only a sardonic laugh for this scenario: *"Already we have virtually no primary rainforest left. Everything you see here is secondary forest. Thousands of plant and animal species, including the orangutan, can live in them. Here in central Kalimantan alone a single company, called Wilmar, has been given a concession for almost 300,000 hectares and now has the legal right to chop down the entire forest. They've already cleared half of it."* From atop a wooden watchtower we looked out over barren terrain: not a single forest tree as far as the eye could see, just kilometer-long rows of freshly planted oil palm saplings. Here and there between the neat rows we noticed the charred remains of a tree trunk. This was Nordin's homeland: *"Take a look around you – how can something like this be sustainable? The WWF shares the blame for the annihilation of our rainforests."*

No legislation, no local resistance, no international protest has succeeded in stopping the advance of the palm oil companies on Indonesia and Malaysia. Great apes and other animals that don't flee the slash-and-burn deforestation operations in time go up in flames along with their forest homes. Many of these forests grow on moorland, and when the forest is burnt down the peat layer, which can be up to 12 meters thick, burns along with it. Thus Indonesia now has the dubious distinction of being one of the world's biggest CO_2 polluters. But de-

Young oil palms with burning rainforest on a Wilmar plantation, 2011

spite its dirty origins, biofuel from palm oil is still considered a *"climate-friendly"* energy source, because the Intergovernmental Panel on Climate Change (IPCC) doesn't factor the greenhouse gases emitted during production of the product into the calculation – in other words, the ecological books are cooked.

Nordin, a man of few words, is a Dayak: one of the indigenous peoples of Borneo. His ancestors were cannibals, which he sometimes reminded me of when he got tired of all my questions. We drove on through the plantations, our jeep swallowed up in dust clouds on the endless red sandy roads. How was it possible that we didn't sink down into the moorland peat? Nordin stopped and showed me how the plantation roadways are made: the remains of the massacred rainforest are laid down like planks, covered with sand, and: hey, presto! A road. The view from the jeep was fatiguing: nothing but oil palms, rows and rows, standing at attention like a silent army.

Machetes are used to chop off the red palm fruits, which lay in huge piles along the roadside. Harvesting them is a laborious business, but it pays off, because palm oil fetches a good price on the global commodities market. Palm oil is an ingredient in thousands of consumer household goods, from soaps, cosmetics and detergents to margarine and sweets. But since Europeans have been sold on the idea of palm oil as a *"renewable"* fuel for vehicles and power plants, the pressure on Indonesia's forests has increased exponentially. The little red fruits have an impressive energy yield – ten times as high as the competition: the soy bean.

Nothing creeps, crawls, buzzes and bites at all anymore in the fields of pristine palm rows. Universal herbicides, pesticides, fungicides and insecticides have eliminated all other plant and animal life. Confronted with these images I asked myself how on earth the WWF could possibly call this industrial monoculture *"sustainable"*. Nordin had no idea either.

Companies like Wilmar International are so big that they have the power to just bulldoze over anything that stands in the way of their growth. The corporation, headquartered in Singapore, has 90,000 employees on the payroll. US industrial agricultural giant Archer Daniels Midland (ADM), the world's largest producer of soy, maize, wheat and cocoa, is the majority shareholder in the company. Wilmar destroys more rainforest in Asia than anyone else. And yet, in 2007 the WWF signed a fixed-term contract to provide the company with pro-bono consultation until 2009. In the words of WWF representative Amalia Prameswari, this was done in the hope of getting Wilmar to *"improve"* its behavior. According to Ms. Prameswari, the WWF wanted to convince the company to produce only *"good palm oil"*.

In the Fairytale Forest

We had met up with Amalia Prameswari before our journey to the dark heart of Borneo's palm oil industry. Arriving for our appointment at WWF Indonesia headquarters in Jakarta's elegant business district, the young woman introduced herself as the Palm Oil Officer responsible for the collaboration with the palm oil companies. She was not overjoyed with the interview; she found the questions too *"political"*. One of the directors should actually have fielded our questions, but they had all made themselves scarce. Amalia made a valiant effort to praise the positive aspects of the *"dialogue"*: *"We give assistance to the companies in how they can implement sustainable activities in their plantations. We also provide training in the implementation of better management practices. We want to mainstream the certification of palm oil sustainability."*[31]

She was sincerely convinced that Wilmar *"with the help of the WWF"* was making *"good progress on the way to sustainable palm oil production"*. How would she define that? *"Wilmar has made a commitment to us to preserve the especially high conservation-value areas. That's a big success of the WWF."* Amalia Prameswari must have registered a certain amount of skepticism in our expressions and encouraged us to: *"Take a look at it for yourselves."*

That was an offer we weren't about to refuse. We took off in Nordin's jeep, driving for hours on the monotonous dusty roads that cut through the plantations like grid lines. Without GPS we would have soon lost all sense of direction. The concessions that Wilmar had secured there, in the heart of Borneo, cover an area over 90 kilometers long about 30 kilometers wide – 271,000 hectares in total. At the time of our visit, almost half of that had already been cleared and planted with oil palms. Thanks to the efforts of the WWF, Amalia Prameswari had told us in parting, 12,000 hectares had been saved from destruction – a whopping 9.86 percent of the concession that had thus far been exploited. The sections considered especially worthy of protection have been dubbed High Conservation Value (HCV) Areas. In its 2007 accord with the WWF, Wilmar had originally agreed to preserve 17,990 hectares of its concession; that's 14.76 percent. A scant year later the company had already made short work of a full third of the promised conservation area. At a joint meeting with the WWF on November 10th, 2008 Wilmar openly admitted the fact.[32] As a result of that round of negotiations the Malaysian office of the global consultancy firm MEC submitted a *"revised"* recommendation to the palm oil multinational. I took a good look at the report, compiled in 2009: half of the so-called HCV areas, which the WWF was convinced had not been cleared subsequent to the original agreement, turned out to be swampland with very high water levels – not really suitable for oil palm plantations anyway. The forests where the indigenous locals live and farm, which don't even belong to Wilmar, had been classed among the HCV areas, as had the lakes, the rivers and the already legally-protected floodplains. Canals used to irrigate peat moors had also been lumped into this key statistic.[33] According to the criteria laid down by the Round Table for Sustainable Palm Oil it is perfectly permissible to include all these areas in the HCV total.

All just smoke and mirrors, as far as Nordin was concerned. Many of the HCV areas listed, he said, were just *"scrub"*, with no value for biodiversity. He gave me a map that he had gotten from the project office of Wilmar itself. There is no date on it, but it's most likely from 2008. The map shows the entire concession area, within which Wilmar had designated only three distinct contiguous sections of forest as *"conservation areas"*: 2,752 hectares along the Pukun River; 2,205 hectares along the Kapuk River; and 196 hectares along the Seranau Kiri.[34] That's a total of 5,153 hectares. All three of the forest areas are river floodplains, which enjoy legal protection in Indonesia anyway. Based on his own on-site observations in this terrain, Nordin believes the Wilmar data is realistic. The WWF, on the other hand, presents satellite images as evidence that their cooperation partner Wilmar had, in fact conserved 13,000 hectares of valuable area.

We were driving through the newly laid out plantation Rimba Harapan Sakti when we were stopped by a Wilmar security jeep. The security officer wanted to know what we were doing there. I asked him where we could find the nearest WWF conservation area. His heavy attitude lightened up and, with a bright mile, he pointed us northwards. A short time later a patch of forest saved from the clearance flames appeared before us in the steamy mists of a recent tropical rain shower. It was like a fata morgana rising up behind a mountain of seedlings, construction machinery, and towering mounds of the root balls of upturned tropical trees. Nordin had surveyed the area a few months earlier: it couldn't have been much more than 80 hectares, i.e. about 900 by 900 meters. You could walk the forest in twenty minutes. It looked plucked and miserable. This was not how I had pictured *"high value"* rainforest. What we had here was quite obviously the secondary forest that had grown back after the clearance twenty years ago. As such, it was of no *"higher value"* than the thousands of hectares of surrounding forest that had been slashed and burned just a few months earlier. A small wooden sign confirmed our suspicions. It read: High Conservation Value Area. Below that, a warning notice stated that it was prohibited to hunt or plant agricultural crops in the forest, and indeed even to enter it.

Suddenly we looked up to see an orangutan at the top of a tree. He looked emaciated as he stared out across the barren land. Almost the exact forlorn look as his cousin from the WWF commercial. All he could see was a parched, brown wasteland; his little patch of remaining forest was an isolated biotope in a sea of oil palms. Would he be able to survive here? Nordin shook his head: *"According to our last survey there are only two orangutans left living here. They don't stand a chance; they're caught in a trap here. Primate researchers say that an orangutan family needs about 10,000 hectares to be able to find enough food and to procreate. There aren't even enough fruit trees in this forest for two apes."*

A few plantation workers came by on bicycles. They stopped, knowing immediately what we were after: Europeans were always interested in the human-like great apes, but seldom in humans. The men were friendly and forthcoming, nonetheless: yes, they knew the orangutans, but they would soon starve to death. In desperation the apes had been going into the plantations and *"stealing"* oil palm fruit or pulling up the palm saplings. I asked what the repercussions were. The workers laughed, then one of them said quietly: *"The company protects its property."* Nordin pursued the point until the man finally stated what we all knew already: *"The company hires hunters to shoot them. They're going to die – one way or the other."*

We wanted to know if the WWF was doing anything to protect the last two orangutans in the forest. The men gave us a blank look: *"We've never seen any of their people around here."* Nordin explained: *"The WWF doesn't have any orangutan projects in Indonesia; it doesn't run any rescue centers where the animals could find shelter."*

Responding to our query, Martina Fleckenstein, Director of EU Policy, Agriculture & Sustainable Biomass of WWF Germany, confirmed that the WWF does not, in fact, maintain a single orangutan rescue station.[35] However, she was at pains to stress that the WWF was involved in rehabilitating forest areas in Sabangau National Park and elsewhere, and was thus indirectly also creating new habitats for the orangutans. The trouble with that is: most orangutans don't live in the country's few national parks; they live in the secondary forests that are currently disappearing in quick succession. According to surveys conducted by the Indonesian Greenomics Institute, six out of nine orangutan habitats in the new Wilmar plantation areas have already been destroyed.[36] Would the company

Palm oil fruits

still receive the coveted certification from the Round Table for Sustainable Palm Oil? Nordin had to laugh: *"Nothing is easier than that – everyone gets it."*

We asked the workers what they thought of their employer Wilmar. The cheerful laughter went silent. A few of them cast anxious sideward glances; one of them said what he really thought: *"I'm a Dayak, from around here. My family used to have land. We lived from its many fruits; everything grew there in abundance. We were able to sell a large part of the harvest at market. Now everything has been destroyed. Even if you were to pull up all of the oil palms again, it would be useless. The soil is contaminated, the earth infertile. It would take decades before anything could grow here again."*

In the distance we saw dark brown smoke clouds. When we got closer we saw that the forest was going up in flames. It was rainforest that the WWF and Wilmar

WWF campaign

had also declared to be *"high value"* and thus should have been protected. Apparently the company was not even sticking to the modest promises it had made to the WWF.

Greenwashing

The WWF reacts sensitively to criticism of its close relationship with the palm oil industry. The national government and not they had determined the land use designations, after all. And if the companies had been granted concessions, their rainforest clearance activities were legal. Furthermore, Indonesia had a right to *"economic development"*. No one could put a stop to the advance of industrial monocultures, the WWF argues, but by maintaining a dialogue with the companies one could enforce *"better"* management decisions. Pursuing this strategy, the WWF joined forces in 2004 with the multinational food giant Unilever, inviting the key corporate industrial players – producers and traders – to their Round Table on Sustainable Palm Oil (RSPO).

The organization is headquartered in Zurich. In the meantime over 500 companies – producers, traders, and financiers – have signed on as fee-paying members of the RSPO. The list includes such luminaries as Bayer, Cargill, DuPont, Henkel, Mitsubishi, Nestlé, Shell, ADM, IKEA, Unilever, Rabobank, HSBC Bank and the energy giant RWE. All of them are on board because the *"sustainable"* label spells profit. Not only that, but since the EU Renewable Energy Act came into effect in 2010, recognized *"sustainability"* certification has been a prerequisite for selling palm oil on the European biofuel market.

The WWF is a member of the RSPO management board and has worked together with its corporate partners from the sector to develop international standards. Whoever fulfills them is granted the sought after seal of sustainability. Nordin says the RSPO certificate can't be taken seriously. His organization, Friends of the Earth, ceased to participate in the Round Table soon after its founding – ditto Greenpeace. *"You can't just go along with such a clear-cut case of fraudulent labeling,"* said Nordin. *"There is no such thing as sustainable monoculture – because it gives the forest no chance of regenerating itself; except for a few last remnants, the forest is simply destroyed."*

Nordin cited the brief list of RSPO fundamentals; a collection of feel-good no-brainers: slavery and child labor are forbidden; pesticides and other chemicals must be stored *"appropriately"*. But the clearance of rainforests is allowed to continue, as long as it doesn't affect *"primary rainforests"*. No real hindrance for the companies, because that still leaves about 9 million hectares that were cleared before the agreement took effect in 2005 – a precautionary measure, so to speak.

Companies that go in now to clear these same areas can still get sustainability certification, no problem. But Nordin believes, based on experience, that even the actual primordial rainforest isn't safe from the chainsaws: *"Even companies that violate RSPO standards, for example by clearing primary forest areas, get their certificate."* The law of the jungle truly applies here. There is no independent oversight authority to ensure that the companies comply with the standards, which are not legally binding but simply a voluntary commitment made by industry.

We wanted to visit a plantation that was in the process of being certified. On the way there Nordin told us about a private conversation he had once had with a palm oil company Sustainability Manager: *"I asked him if he could show me the difference between a sustainable plantation and a normal one. He just said: what difference?"*

We drove about 20 kilometers to our destination: the Kerry Sawit plantation. It, too, belongs to Wilmar International Limited. There we saw full-grown oil palms heavy with dense clusters of oil fruit. The trees require five years of growth before the fruit can be harvested for the first time – a long time to wait for a company itching to turn a profit with the oil. At the time, the Kerry Sawit plantation was in the middle of the certification procedure. The German Technical Inspection Association, TÜV Rheinland, does the technical evaluations. It's a good contract: a single certification costs around 70,000 dollars. Only big multinational corporations can afford to play ball; small local producers are thus virtually locked out of the *"certified sustainable palm oil"* market.

As soon as we jumped out of the jeep we had to hold our noses. The biting stench of untreated wastewater from an oil mill was overwhelming. The effluent runs through open trenches and then sinks directly into the ground, and has also contaminated the nearby river. The plantation would most likely receive the green seal of approval nonetheless; it seems that Indonesian law is blind when it comes to a partner as mighty as Wilmar.

Nordin, sitting looking lost and forlorn near a toxic green effluent lake, said: *"What is the WWF thinking? This cannot possibly be sustainable. Nothing grows here at all anymore. There is no biodiversity in the plantations; everything is dead. Rats are the only animals left here. The WWF greenwashes the environmental crimes of industry – and even takes money for doing it."*

The WWF as a Business Model

During our inspection of the plantation we came upon a chemicals canister labeled: Paraquat. What was the toxic substance doing there? Paraquat has achieved notoriety as one of the most dangerous herbicides on earth and has been banned in Europe via a decision of the European Court of Justice. Even a minuscule amount of the Swiss-made product is deadly, and its use is prohibited in Switzerland as well. Thousands of plantation workers across the globe have already died or suffer severe long-term health damage from inhaling the Paraquat fumes. Because of this fallout even the big banana producers Chiquita and Dole now prohibit the use of the herbicide on their plantations. But was it allowed here? On a *"sustainable"* palm oil plantation?

According to the standards set by the Round Table for Sustainable Palm Oil, use of poisonous substances should be reduced on the plantations. The document states: *"The use of herbicides and pesticides must not endanger human beings or the environment."* Yet Paraquat use is permitted, and the Swiss company Syngenta that produces it is a paying member of the Round Table and an official partner of the WWF. Coincidence?

In June 2011 a concerned contributor to a WWF online discussion forum asked why the WWF wasn't using the Round Table to push for a ban on Paraquat. The answer from the central office of WWF Germany speaks for itself: *"Palm oil producers who are members of the RSPO need a plan to show them how they can reduce, or even eliminate, the use of such substances ... Furthermore, it has to be said that Paraquat is not the 'core business' of the WWF at the RSPO. We've focused our attention on the extremely critical issue of deforestation."* What this statement implies, of course, is that human rights are not the "core business" of the WWF either.

Germany-based global detergent giant Henkel is another member of the Round Table whose membership fees have already paid off: when the company launched its new product line Terra Activ, which was on the market from 2008 to 2014, it prominently bore the green palm label. The target group was conscientious consumers who want to do something to help the rainforest, and are prepared to pay a few cents more to do so. In addition to the green palm *"seal of sustainability"* on the label of the new cleaning products, concerned customers were given the reassuring information: *"Terra Activ unites powerful strength and nature in a formula based on renewable raw materials, for shiny clean surfaces. Today's way to clean. Terra Activ supports RSPO-certified sustainable palm oil production ..."*

The palm oil industry is not only busy destroying the last major rainforest areas in Indonesia; in Africa, as well as Central and South America, immense tracts of land are being bought up to expand the booming business with the precious vegetable oil. The more biofuel is used in the Northern Hemisphere, the better the climate results presented by European governments will look – at least on paper. The countries of the earth's Southern Hemisphere pay the high price of this eco-scam. For these vast regions the upswing in the bioenergy sector not only spells the loss of arable land for food crops, it also means the death of local smallholder farming and the entire culture that goes with it. Again and again WWF staff assured me that the organization was only involved in order to prevent *"even worse things"* from happening. Nordin dismisses this argument; it just doesn't hold water: *"The WWF is an integral part of the whole. The RSPO's sustainability swindle wouldn't even work without the WWF – they're what gives the whole thing credibility. It's a nasty business."*

The PR buzzwords on the Henkel website give credence to the Indonesian activist's statement: *"Henkel, together with the WWF, is thus supporting the sustainable production of palm and palm-kernel oil. In this way the company is making a valuable contribution to protecting the rainforest."* That sounds like music to conscientious consumer ears, but the moving strains of this green hymn easily distract attention from a discordant fact: the rainforest that Henkel is ostensibly helping to protect must first be completely destroyed. Only then can the land where it had stood be used for palm oil production ennobled with the *"sustainable"* label.

The Henkel website also states that since 2003 the company has *"supported the WWF in its campaign for the Indonesian rainforest"*. The WWF has come up with its own inventive way of rewarding the *"support"*: with an international competition for the best palm oil purchaser. In 2011 Henkel scored nine out of nine possible points on the WWF *"Buyers' Scorecard"* – a world-class result. So both backs get scratched.

An alliance with the WWF offers corporations like Henkel a cost-effective method of greenwashing their business activities and public image. This organized use of sustainability certification as a currency for selling indulgences has disastrous consequences: the system actually helps big agribusiness to avoid changing its behavior. As long as consumers and politicians in Europe and the USA continue to fall for the fraudulent labeling, the industrial players will have a green light to keep speeding ahead on the road to ecological ruin.

A Night in Sembuluh

From time to time we crossed paths with a transport truck laden with red oil fruit on its way to the next oil mill. Every few kilometers we passed a settlement of the low barracks that house the plantation workers. At the entrance to one of these camps we discovered a wooden plaque bearing the eight *"guiding principles"* defined by the Round Table for Sustainable Palm Oil:

1. Commitment to transparency
2. Compliance with applicable laws and regulations
3. Commitment to long-term economic and financial viability
4. Use of appropriate best practices by growers and millers
5. Environmental responsibility and conservation of natural resources and biodiversity
6. Responsible consideration of employees, smallholders and other individuals and communities affected by growers and mills
7. Responsible development of new plantings
8. Commitment to continuous improvement in key areas of activity

Nordin said he found some of the RSPO fundamentals quite sensible: *"In the implementation provisions of the sixth principle it says, for example, that the land rights of the local population must be respected. That's good. Unfortunately it doesn't work in practice, because the Indonesian state is not actually based on the rule of law. The WWF chooses to ignore our political reality and in this way dodges its own responsibility."* Suddenly a Wilmar security vehicle appeared behind us and Nordin stepped on the gas. The whole area is private company property.

At nightfall we arrived at the village Sembuluh by a lake of the same name. Many of the villagers live in traditional lakeshore houses on stilts. Some of the fishermen were still out on their boats; everywhere along the wooden piers at water's edge people were crouched down washing cloth or showering themselves with river water from a bucket – until the call of the muezzin put a halt to these mundane activities: the entire population of Sembuluh is Muslim.

Until three years before our visit most of the villagers had been farmers, cultivating the traditional forest crops of the Dayak: rattan for furniture, and rubber trees. The profits were good because, despite competition from synthetics, high-quality condoms and chewing gum are still made of natural caoutchouc. Between the trees of these staple crops the smallholders had planted rice and fruit trees: durian, mango and banana. A mixed forest habitat in which the animals also felt at home; a truly sustainable economy that provided a good living for the local population.

The forest smallholdings now exist only in the memory of the farmers; their forest gardens have long since been bulldozed away. In Indonesia, forest per se belongs to the state. As a rule, farmers have only usage rights. But some of them were in possession of legitimate title deeds. The corporation would have to buy the land from such individuals. In the expectation of sudden wealth, many of the inhabitants of Sembuluh had, in fact, sold up. They now cruised the main street of the village in their newly bought motor scooters, or rode them to work each morning at one of the plantations that now surround the village.

Hadid, who kindly allowed us to spend the night in his attic, had not sold. As we sat eating dinner on the floor of his kitchen he explained why: *"The money is soon spent and the company only employs people until the age of 45. What do they do after that? It was stupid to sell."* Hadid tends to his forest smallholding daily. A few of the farmers who had sold their land were now working for him. His wife runs the village hardware store. Hadid is a wealthy and respected man; people here heed his word.

That evening his house was full of local farmers, gathered to plan a protest activity. By that time there were three oil mills on the lakeshore, contaminating the lake with their effluent. The farmers feared that the fish would all die. Fishing was one of their last remaining sources of income, and the most important source of protein for the villagers. Nordin followed the discussion while typing the first sentences of a petition into Hadid's computer. The plan was for all to travel to the provincial capital the following Monday. There they would make a personal appeal to the Governor to stop construction of a fourth oil mill due to be built near the lake.

Just as the discussion had reached fever pitch Nordin's cell phone beeped: a text message from an anonymous caller: *"We know you're in Sembuluh. Get lost now, or we'll get rid of you once and for all. We can find you anywhere. The governor and the police are on our side."* Nordin is highly unpopular with the corporations: he foments unrest among the farmers and puts a damper on business. He closed the SMS screen with a shrug; it wasn't the first death threat he had received.

Baktaran, a gaunt farmer in his mid-forties, showed me the deed to a parcel of forestland: five hectares that had belonged to his parents before him. *"But the company bribed the officials and I lost everything."* Had he just accepted his fate? In lieu of an answer he asked if I would go with him early the next morning to see his forest.

At sunrise we started off on foot into the underbrush. Baktaran cleared the way ahead of us with his machete. Suddenly he stopped and said abruptly: *"Here we are. This is my garden."* But all we saw was scrub and in it oil palms about 1.5 meters tall. *"They came one morning with bulldozers and destroyed my forest. There was a huge rubber tree right here – I had inherited it from my father. I went to the Wilmar administration office to complain – they just threw me out."* Between the palms Baktaran had erected a little ramshackle hut out of wood and palm fronds; a symbolic demonstration of his claim to ownership: *"I've kept coming back here, almost every day, for five years now. Once, the company sent the military to get rid of me, but I won't give up."*

Baktaran then marched over to the next oil palm and chopped it down with a few precision whacks of his machete. That was destruction of company property – a crime under Indonesian law. Other farmers were currently in prison for doing the same thing, more than 300 of them throughout the country.

A few weeks after our interview with Baktaran I received word that after a five-year legal battle the farmer had received justice. Wilmar had lost the case and would have to return the land to its rightful owner – oil palms and all. A rare triumph of the rule of law.

The Palm Oil War

Amalia Prameswari, the WWF palm oil functionary we had met with in Jakarta, defended herself against the accusation of collusion with companies engaged in criminal activities. She admitted that even a modern company like Wilmar didn't always act properly, but at least it had promised the WWF to protect the rainforest *"as far as possible"*: *"There is enough degraded land in Indonesia to treble palm oil production without having to destroy any more rainforest."* Prameswari quoted a statistic to back up her statement: five to seven million hectares lay fallow in Indonesia. But where were these enormous tracts of land?

On our travels throughout the country we had not seen a single hectare that was not being exploited somehow by someone. The young WWF official attempted a careful retraction: *"It's a tough challenge. Most of the time the land belongs to someone, and then conflicts occur. These have to be resolved through mutual agreement. We reject illegal and one-sided initiatives where people are displaced. The Roundtable wants amicable solutions."*

We showed her film footage from a provincial prison in Sumatra: 16 farmers cooped up in a tiny cell like battery hens. They were all from Jambi Province and had been accused of stealing oil fruit from the land that had belonged to them for decades. The men looked exhaust-

Imprisoned farmer in Sumatra

ed as they stood behind the bars asking for help. One of them said: *"Who'll feed my children now? Help us; we're desperate. They're never going to let us out of here."*

Amalia Prameswari was visibly moved by the farmer's words. She swallowed hard: *"Well, me personally, I have not heard about this case until today. It would be a disappointment, of course, if Wilmar has really let such a thing happen. On the other hand, they also have other sustainability practices in other areas of Indonesia."* Apparently, Wilmar was not always Wilmar. As if trying hard to reassure herself, she added: *"The WWF only supports good bioenergy."*

This, however, was no comfort to the captive farmers, all members of the Suku Anak Dalam tribe. A few months after the prison interview was recorded the tribe's conflict with Wilmar had escalated, climaxing in an orgy of violence: on August 15th, 2011 Wilmar subsidiary PT

Asiatic Persada called in paramilitary units to dispel the rebellious inhabitants of Sungai Buayan village, located in the middle of the company's palm oil plantation. Three hundred armed militiamen surrounded the settlement and opened fire on the unarmed inhabitants, who fled in panic. The villagers had ensconced themselves there in the firm belief it was their land –Wilmar had robbed them of it 9 years earlier.

Ida, a mother of four, had been cooking at the stove when the shots rang out: *"I was making rice. To protect my children I threw the rice at the soldiers. Several people collapsed from gunshot wounds and had to be operated on. After the attack, the soldiers came with heavy vehicles and flattened our huts. They destroyed everything we had: our food reserves, our clothing. We don't know how we'll survive now."*

The petite, friendly woman from the rainforest told me this story on board a little passenger boat as it tugged up the Weser River in the northern German town of Brake. Four months had past since the raid on her village, and the tribe had sent Ida, her husband Bidin and their youngest son Agung off to faraway Europe to tell the people here about the price the indigenous forest dwellers are being forced to pay for the palm oil used in European industries. In a last ditch attempt to prevent the delegation from travelling to Europe, Wilmar had offered to build replacement housing for the villagers, in a worker's settlement off the plantation grounds. *"What would we do there? We don't want handouts; we want our land back."* Nothing productive had come of negotiations with Wilmar, just *"empty promises"* – and two sacks of rice. Company managers had dropped them off in her village just before Christmas: two sacks for 700 people.

Our boat, with the victims of the violent raid in Sumatra on board, was nearing the industrial port of Brake, the site of a modern Wilmar-run vegetable oil refinery. It pumps out 2,500 tons of refined oil a day for use in margarine, cosmetics and cleaning products. The logo of the global concern could be seen from a distance at the top of the main building. Ida couldn't read the sign – she's illiterate. Her husband Bidin spelled out the name and shook with rage: *"That's the same name as on the sign in front of our village – right in the middle of our forest, on the land of our ancestors. And then it says: 'This land is the property of Wilmar – no trespassing!'"* He looked up at the smoke billowing out of the refinery chimney and then finished his thought: *"And all of that just to make margarine here out of our forest."*

The emaciated yet tough, strong-willed man had begun to contemplate the strange ways of globalization on our drive to the river through the Weser marshlands. On both sides of the road he saw lush meadows and the steam of cow dung rising from the big low stalls into the cold December air. *"Why"*, Bidin had asked me, *"don't you just eat butter, when there are so many cows here? Why do have to eat margarine even though it's destroying our lives?"*

Bidin had never before left his forest home. He shivered with cold on our boat ride across the wind-whipped Weser. What tormented him most was the thought of his children's future: *"They can't play outdoors any more; the brown soup with all the chemicals flows everywhere, throughout the plantation. The children get sick or die just by touching something. I can no longer show them how to climb a rubber tree or how to make rattan furniture. We're losing the knowledge that we've gathered over centuries."*

The plantation that had been erected on Bidin's tribal lands would soon receive sustainability certification. But that won't bring his forest back. Will the margarine taste better to us with *"from sustainable production"* on the label?

Ida with child and husband Bidin on a boat trip

7. Eco-Indulgences for Sale

The World Ethanol & Biofuels Conference was being held at the luxury Hotel Intercontinental in Geneva. A few hundred managers from the booming bioenergy sector had come to the posh Swiss venue to discuss new technologies and marketing strategies. The industry players had invited the head of the WWF biomass section from Berlin to give her expert input on the marketing side; in an elegant black blazer she looked right at home among all the slick corporate "suits". Before going to work for the WWF she had been the assistant to the Managing Director of the German Bioethanol Association. Due to a court settlement I am no longer allowed to refer to this woman by name. Madam "X" took the conference stage and proceeded to push the schmooze button: *"We're different than other conservancy groups – we're constructive."* Companies that acquired the WWF-approved certificate for *"sustainable"* biofuel, she said, would be on the safe side and *"continue to do brilliant business"*. And she had another piece of *"good news"*: The WWF was in favor of *"appropriating"* even more lands worldwide than previously for fuel crops – a welcome message that was greeted with friendly applause from the delegates in the hall.

After her speech I approached the WWF speaker as she mingled with the crowd. Not only am I prevented for legal reasons from naming her here, I am likewise unable to quote the justification she gave for the WWF closing ranks with industry. Ms. Biomass has accomplished this neat bit of censorship with a decision made by the District Court of Cologne. The grounds: the interview was conducted for my film 'The Silence of the Pandas', but she had never explicitly agreed to the publication of her statements in book form.

The Philanthropic Bank

The HSBC Bank building, an imposing palace of glass and steel in London's Canary Wharf business district, has been dubbed the city's most expensive property. The Hongkong and Shanghai Banking Corporation, or HSBC, was founded in 1865, and is Europe's biggest bank. It is the financial heart of the palm oil industry, pumping billions into its business bloodstream. HSBC has also contributed 100 million dollars to a climate protection program – a joint project with the WWF. It would be churlish, of course, to suggest an unsavory connection.

Francis Sullivan, head of the bank's Sustainability Department, greeted me on one of the upper floors. Before Sullivan's rise to the heights of the HSBC tower he had been Director of Conservation at WWF UK. His change of employer, said Sullivan with a hint of pride in his voice, had *"solidified"* the good relations between HSBC and the WWF, which were based on a *"strategical partnership"*. His bank was now the *"greenest"* in the world: *"The skyscraper you're in right now is carbon-neutral."*

No bank on earth has financed more loans in the new biofuel energy sector than HSBC. *"We believe in renewable energy"*, said Sullivan emphatically, *"and we're prepared to share the responsibility for it."* This new green gold is a high-risk business: the palm oil fruit have to grow for five years before they can produce their first yields. The corporations need a lot of money to bridge the time gap, which is where HSBC or the World Bank steps in. The WWF is a strategic partner of both financial institutions. They need the trusted image of the panda brand to win over a worldwide public skeptical of the controversial biofuels industry.

Francis Sullivan found this hypothesis *"very bold"*. My critical remark about the gigantic HSBC *"contribution"* to the WWF likewise rolled off him like oil on Teflon: *"The 100 million dollars were not a reward for the WWF. It was a perfectly ordinary philanthropic donation. Together with the WWF and other partners we want to use the money to protect the world's great rivers, for instance the Yangtze."* Did Mr. Sullivan believe it was possible to influence WWF policy with financial donations? *"The WWF can't be bought. But you should ask them yourself; I can't speak for them."*

In terms of the palm oil industry, Sullivan said, the bank did follow a strategy coordinated in conjunction with the WWF: *"The job we do is similar to that of the WWF. We too want to see sustainability become the predominant business principle. When customers from the palm oil industry want loans we strongly recommend that they convert their production to conform to the standards of the Round Table, RSPO. We take our responsibility very seriously. Anyone who breaks the rules won't get another loan from us."*

Had that ever happened before? Francis Sullivan did not want to say – banking confidentiality. I asked if it wasn't agonizing for him, as a former professional environmentalist, to see the palm oil industry using his bank's money to burn down the rainforests of Indonesia and Malaysia. Sullivan nodded in complete sympathy with my pedantic concerns: *"The certification system is new, so it's not yet perfect, but from our point of view it's a good start. We're working on it."* I gave it another try: *"Millions of hectares of forest have been cleared with slash and burn methods that result in massive carbon emissions. Your bank financed that. You were a professional conservationist for many years, does that really leave you cold?"* Francis Sullivan was British composure itself as he launched into his reply: *"Those are backward-looking questions – let's talk instead about how we can join together to solve the problems of the present."* I gave up. The metamorphosis from WWF director to bank manager had clearly been a total success.

An Uprising in Sumatra

Feri Irawan is a professional land surveyor. With his long flowing hair he looks a bit like an Indonesian Che Guevara. He implicates two international players as accessories to the crimes against humanity being committed in his country Sumatra in the name of sustainability: *"The HSBC Bank and the WWF provide international cover for the often criminal activities of the palm oil companies in our homeland. It's no coincidence that the bank placed 100 million dollars at the disposal of the WWF. With the help of the WWF the industry has succeeded in selling the destructive monoculture to the international markets as 'sustainable'."*

Feri Irawan is seen as the leader of the farmers' rebellion in Sumatra's Jambi province. For the sustainability rhetoric of a Francis Sullivan he had only a disdainful shrug: "*The HSBC Bank says it helps the farmers because it lends them money as part of a program for smallholders. That's true – but the farmers are only given a loan if they use their land to plant oil palms. That leads to even more land being sacrificed for palm oil.*" Feri Irawan showed me a photo: the farmers of his village Karang Mendapo demonstrating outside the Permata Bank, an HSBC subsidiary: "*The bank wants to bring us to ruin. They're demanding we pay back a loan of 88 billion rupiah.*"

Feri Irawan, Jambi on Sumatra

That's 10 million dollars. The farmers were supposed to pay back a loan taken out by the palm oil company Sinar Mas. The company had invested the bank's money in a new plantation built right smack in the middle of land belonging to farmers in Feri Irawan's home village Karang Mendapo. That was in 2003. Sinar Mas, which has close personal and political ties to the government, had literally banked on the fact that it would be able to keep the land. But the local smallholders did not cave in, occupying their own stolen land in protest. They also took their case to court. In 2008, after a five-year legal battle, a civil court decided in favour of the farmers: Sinar Mas was ordered to give them back their land.

"From the palm oil industry's perspective the victory of the village is dangerous because it could be a template for resistance throughout Indonesia," said Feri Irawan, *"that's why the company is hitting back – to make an example of us."* The new mayor Muhamad Rusdi, one of the leaders of the farmers' uprising, had been brutally beaten by hired thugs and had to be given police protection. A few months later Rusdi had been arrested by the same police force. Following an *"anonymous tip-off"* they had found a stack of money in his office, allegedly *"graft"*. The mayor was found to be completely innocent before a court of law. Someone had planted the money in his office to discredit him.

Feri Irawan thought that because its terror and intimidation tactics had failed, the company was now resorting to the payment demands to bring the farmers to their knees. The HSBC Bank was of the legal opinion that the farmers were liable for the loan repayment because they had been the beneficiaries of the investment – albeit involuntarily. Feri Irawan could see no solution to the conflict: *"The farmers barely stand a chance in court, but there's no way they can pay; how could they possibly raise such an enormous sum of money? The loan hangs like a sword of Damocles over the village."*

"I'm actually a conservationist," said Feri Irawan, as if he had to remind himself of the fact from time to time. The co-founder of Friends of the Earth Sumatra could hardly find the time anymore for his main pursuit: trying to protect the endangered orangutan and tiger populations. The *"palm oil mafia"* had forced him into active

political resistance. He believed that the farmers and indigenous tribes would only stand a chance if they banded together to fight for their rights.

It was clear to Feri Irawan that the *"greenwashing policies"* of the WWF promote the palm oil industry's business. In every conflict, the default position of the organization had been to side with the corporations and never with the farmers. The deals made between the palm oil industry, the provincial government and the WWF had produced the positive perk of two new national parks in his homeland Sumatra, but this couldn't reconcile Irawan with the WWF: *"The national parks are part of a plan for land use, which involved the government and the WWF plotting out the division of our country behind closed doors: the majority of the land was earmarked for clearance, and a couple of national parks were created as a fig leaf. The trouble is, the people in the park areas are being displaced as well. I experienced it first-hand in Kerinci Seblat National Park: the WWF and the World Bank had together mapped out the borders of the park. Tens of thousands of people were resettled. I can testify to the fact that even after the mass resettlement of the inhabitants rainforest was still being cleared within the national park. Even tiger numbers continued to sink. The project is a complete failure. In the end, the locals were so enraged that they started setting the cars of the WWF functionaries on fire."*

Sumatra offers rich spoils. After exploiting the country's tropical woods and palm oil, agribusinesses had discovered a lucrative new sector: the trade in carbon credits. Here too the WWF offers its valuable consultation services. It goes like this: companies that clear forests for industry but conserve a few especially high-value areas are rewarded with credits for *"avoided carbon emissions"*. This carbon offset system is a product of the United Nations REDD program (reducing emissions from deforestation and forest degradation), a participant in the Intergovernmental Panel on Climate Change (IPCC). The carbon credits can then be sold for cash value on the Paris climate exchange.

There is another attractive option for making money with climate issues that is also very popular: palm oil industry players who invest in *"climate-friendly technologies"* can receive carbon credits from a further UN program, the Clean Development Mechanism (CDM). Under this scheme, Wilmar, for example, gets carbon offsets and renewable energy certificates (RECs) for running its oil mills on palm oil instead of diesel.

As if all that weren't enough, agribusiness came up with a *"third way"* of trading on the climate for cash: Sinar Mas, Wilmar, Cargill & Co. decided that activities such as planting oil palms on fallow forest areas or on land that had been deforested beforehand should be recognized as *"reforestation initiatives"*. These would be rewarded with yet more RECs, thank you very much.

In 2010 this absurd and audacious idea was actually introduced as a bill before the European Commission.

The EU Commission withdrew the bill in response to massive protest from environmental NGOs, but the reforestation idea as such is still being floated, and there's a good chance it could still be officially recognized by the World Climate Council. According to the criteria of the UN Food and Agriculture Organization (FAO) it is, in fact, acceptable to define a palm oil plantation as *"forest"*: the mature trees grow to over 5 meters tall and the crowns of the trees overshadow at least 10 percent of the *"forest"* floor. With that, all classification criteria are fulfilled. Thus the palm oil industry could, in the end, finally get its sought-after carbon credit rewards for tireless efforts in annihilating the earth's green lungs.

Certification: We Can Get It for You Wholesale

Despite intensive and costly PR campaigns the Round Table for Sustainable Palm Oil has suffered a setback. The terror tactics applied against the civilian population, plus images of the Indonesian and Malaysian rainforests going up in smoke, have sullied the reputation of palm oil. So much so that many block-type thermal power stations no longer wish to use palm oil from Indonesia or Malaysia, even if it bears the RSPO green palm label. The public pressure has also made the EU Commission more cautious, and in the fall of 2011 it denied approval to the green palm seal in a preliminary decision. The Round Table would have to make its standards more stringent, bringing them in line with EU renewable energies guidelines. The RSPO standards were duly adapted, and in November 2012 the EU did finally approve the green palm certification.

But the industry couldn't wait that long so, luckily for them, their partner WWF still had a wild card left in its hand: a brand new sustainability seal of approval with the cumbersome name International Sustainability and

Carbon Certification, ISCC for short. It is applicable to all biomass products that can be used to produce fuel. The ISCC association is headquartered in Cologne and Martina Fleckenstein from WWF Germany serves as its deputy chairwoman. Sitting beside her on the management board are old acquaintances, including managers from the big agri-multinationals Cargill and ADM. The German Federal Ministry of Food and Agriculture paid the development costs of the certification system and the European Union was astonishingly quick to approve it as suitable *"renewable energy"* validation.

The ISCC standards are nearly identical to those of the RSPO. The only addition is that the new system explicitly cites a climate goal that conforms to the EU guidelines: the use of vegetable oils as fuel must result in a reduction of carbon emissions. The ISCC hit the ground running: within its first few months on the market the limited liability company had already granted its seal of approval to more than 700 biofuel industry companies. The bar for the certification is not set very high – especially for an agribusiness that sits down with the WWF at the Round Table for Sustainable Palm Oil.

Martina Fleckenstein is Director of EU Policy, Agriculture and Sustainable Biomass at WWF Germany and is known as the mother of ISCC certification. She organizes promotional tours to Indonesia, which she uses to personally convince hesitant industrialists of the advantages of "her" seal: *"ISCC is a global system that covers all types of biomass. It applies equally to the EU market area and to overseas. It offers companies all services from a single source, which facilitates international trade."*[37]

The word "nature" is never mentioned. In an interview with the trade publication Top Agrar Martina Fleckenstein gives valuable tips: attaining ISCC certification would be *"no problem"* for companies that already had the (RSPO) certificate in their pocket *"because relevant prerequisites, such as environmental assessments, will have already been fulfilled."*[38]

When queried, ISCC management in Cologne confirmed that in such cases they did not subject producers to their own comprehensive environmental inspections, so that the inspector usually needed just a single day to put a plantation or oil mill through its certification paces. The website for the new ISCC system promotes its seal by stressing the uncomplicated certification process: *"The scope of the evaluation is minimized via group certification processes and via document audits, where sufficient."*[39]

Dr. Jan Henke from the ISCC LLC in Cologne explained to me over the phone what was meant by the cryptic statement: *"When an oil mill is supplied by 100 farmers it isn't feasible to inspect every one of them. For this reason we inspect 10 percent of the producers; 90 percent ensure us via self-declaration that they adhere to the ISCC standards."* But who is there to guarantee that those 90 percent of the producers are telling the truth? *"In some regions that might be the wholesale buyer, for example"* was Dr. Henke's answer. *"The buyer is responsible for confirming to us that suppliers produce in accordance with ISCC criteria."* But how can buyers assess their suppliers? According to Dr. Jan Henke, they had a good grip on that too: *"The buyers either believe what the producers tell them, or they can also make further inquiries or even carry out their own inspection on site."*

Thus the fox is sent to mind the henhouse. Large-scale wholesale buyers, such as Cargill and other global traders in biomass, can use this convenient method to hand their own suppliers a get-out-of-jail-free card. The system is lean, efficient and unbureaucratic: a good deal for every link in the value chain, including, presumably, the WWF, which helps and consults wherever it can.

The ISCC sustainability certificate had just made its debut when, in August 2010, Cargill and the WWF agreed to cooperate in the palm oil business. Cargill is a US grain giant with a workforce of 138,000 and annual profits of around 4 billion dollars. It is, among other things, the biggest palm oil trader in the world and also runs its own plantations. Cargill sources most of its oil fruit, however, from other producers, such as Wilmar and Sinar Mas; in other words, from companies notorious for their ruthless treatment of nature, rainforest farmers and indigenous peoples.

On the Cargill website I found a reference to the partnership agreement with the WWF, the spirit and purpose of which is described as follows: *"Cargill is working with the WWF to undertake an assessment of its palm oil suppliers in Indonesia as part of its continuous commitment to sustainable palm oil production."* They offer their own homespun definition of sustainability as the gold standard in this undertaking: *"We already have responsible palm production policies on our own plantations, and we want to play our part by working with the industry and the Indonesian government to encourage the adoption of sustainable production practices. The collaboration is based on the responsible palm oil production we practice on our own plantations."*

An expert group from the Rainforest Action Network (RAN) investigated to find out how Cargill really runs its production. Between July 2009 and March 2010 the San Francisco-based organization took a forensic look at four Cargill palm oil plantations in Borneo. Their findings were sobering: Cargill had illegally cleared huge areas of rainforest, destroyed peat bogs and expelled local inhabitants. The experts documented evidence that Cargill had broken Indonesian laws and also violated the very Round Table for Sustainable Palm Oil (RSPO) standards it had helped to draft.[40] Not a trace of sustainability to be found.

The WWF sustainability discourse has been chewed over and perfected ad absurdum at so many conferences and media outlets that it has entered the common parlance – not least because of the high credibility ranking of the panda. The certification industry hopes that in all of this a basic fact will somehow be overlooked: a mass industrial monoculture that replaces the rainforest cannot, by definition, be *"sustainable"*. This fundamental contradiction has given rise to some ludicrous PR campaigns.

Cultivating Champions

One of the largest palm oil plantation operators is the Malaysian company Sime Darby. It hired the British agency FBC Media to produce seemingly serious documentary films about the blessings of the sustainable palm oil industry. The aim was to cultivate a few opinion leaders for the cause, as stated in an internal agency concept paper.

FBC Media successfully fulfilled its brief and, by its own admission, *"cultivated five champions"* ready to spring into action for their Malaysian client. At a client presentation the PR agency introduced the PR campaign's five leading propagandists: Prof. Jeffrey Sachs, Director of the Earth Institute in New York; Dr. Tom Maddox of the Zoological Society of London; Dr. Charles McNeill of the UN Development Programme; Prof. Shahid Naeem of Columbia University; and Dr. Jason Clay of the WWF.[41]

The deployment of these heavyweights, it says in the FBC Media presentation, would help to place films and articles in serious media channels. *"The FBC campaign is helping to cement Sime Darby's reputation as a conservation-minded industry leader."* The agency won't reveal the fees of the campaign *"champions"*. Prof. Sachs' Earth Institute has publicly admitted that it received a donation of over a half a million dollars from the Sime Darby Company.

I asked WWF *"champion"* Jason Clay if he had also been rewarded for his efforts. His answer came via WWF headquarters in Switzerland:

"Dr. Clay is not a cultivated champion for Sime Darby. He was not engaged in any PR initiative by either Sime Darby or FBC Media, nor has he received any reward from either entity. While he was listed as a target for the firm's efforts, he has not had any involvement in the initiative described in the referenced report."

What the WWF neglected to mention was the fact that the organization has long received direct, regular payments from Sime Darby – for consultation services, on the basis of a contract from November 2010. According to the Malaysian company, the deal was *"An agreement to carry out a study on selected estates to formulate recommendations to improve sustainable plantation management."*[42]

Money is not the only means by which the partnership between the WWF and Sime Darby flourishes; the two also bond via personnel: businesswoman Caroline Russell is a member of the supervisory board of Sime Darby and also treasurer of WWF Malaysia and a member of the WWF Board of Trustees.

FBC-Media did, in fact, succeed in placing its PR films (genre: serious documentary) very advantageously. The tales of the beneficent works of Sime Darby were sold to reputable public broadcast channels such as BBC World. The BBC has since begun an internal investigation to get to the bottom of this scandalous breach of journalistic integrity.[43]

The Broken Heart of Borneo

The WWF is coming under increasing fire from the Asian environmental and human rights movement for tolerating the sins of its partners against human beings and nature – and for taking a direct share of the profits. Doubt about the panda's pure goodness is also growing worldwide. Even organizations that previously worked with the WWF are now distancing themselves. Greenpeace, for example, has publicly described the palm oil sustainability certification as *"a farce"*.[44] The WWF, on the other hand, remains economical with self-criticism. It continues to dish out its warm and cuddly primordial rainforest feel-good story, letting it work its subtle magic on the donating public in the rich developed world.

One of these heart-rending stories is the Heart of Borneo, a WWF prestige project. According to the WWF's own information, the organization had used its good connections to politics and industry to save a rainforest area the size of Great Britain from predatory exploitation. The conservation project Heart of Borneo is transnational, spanning the borders in sections of Indonesia, Brunei and Malaysia. In February 2007, in a move initiated by the WWF, the national governments of the three countries signed a declaration of intent to protect the rainforest region – at the request of the WWF the German federal government picked up the tab.

But there was a catch: the unusual methods that would be used to save the rainforest, clearly revealed in the project description: *"Promotion of investment in the sustainable use of natural resources. This results in an alternative to the previous overexploitation by eco-tourism, in the form of the sustainable production of palm oil and sustainable forest management."*[45] Thus, according to WWF logic, the rainforest can only be protected when it becomes an economic factor, exploited for profit – even if it means destroying it first.

The Heart of Borneo project presents financial contributors in the Northern Hemisphere with an illusory picture of a tropical dream world. But the gruesome reality on the ground is documented in a report by London-based international environmental and human rights organization Global Witness. The group had investigated the practices of the Global Forest and Trade Network (GFTN), a WWF initiative in which it collaborates with 288 timber companies – the world's largest timber alliance. The WWF guarantees that its partners supply only legally and sustainably harvested timber. In July 2011 Global Witness discovered that Malaysia's biggest timber company, Ta Ann Holdings, was systematically destroying rainforest: every day the WWF network member company fells an area of rainforest the size of 20 football fields, destroying orangutan habitat within the boundaries of the Heart of Borneo project as it goes.[46]

We Feed the World

Jason Clay is one of the few senior WWF officials who speaks openly about the organization's close associations with big business – albeit preferably in an intimate setting *"among friends"*, such as a meeting of the Global Harvest Initiative, a lobbyist organization representing agribusiness and GMO giants Cargill, Monsanto, Archer Daniels Midland (ADM) and John Deere. WWF also recently joined the group, and is represented there by Dr. Jason Clay. He is Vice President of WWF USA and also developed the global management network Market Transformation for WWF International. The network manages the relationships between the WWF and multinational corporations. Clay also heads the WWF Aquaculture Network.

Jason Clay is known as a key strategist within WWF, having personally orchestrated the most important international industry partnerships. In the summer of 2010 at the meeting of the Global Harvest Initiative in Washington D.C. Jason Clay talked turkey with his agribusiness brethren, offering them a strategic alliance as a solution to the global food supply problem: projections suggest that by the year 2050 food production will need to double – using less arable land.

According to Clay, this feat can only be achieved by the global food corporations and an industrial form of agriculture, because, he says, over half of the world's smallholders *"can't even feed themselves"* – an assertion that Jason Clay in fact has trouble proving. The governments of these countries, he adds, are also incapable of solving these food problems because they tend towards *"protectionism"*: *"Increasingly, food is a global issue. To be most effective moving forward, we will have to develop global strategies and plans for food security, rather than individual country ones."*[47]

The narrative is this: the agribusiness multinationals must take charge of the entire production and distribution chain, because only then can valuable resources, such as water, land and energy, be conserved. And, according to Clay, only the big global players had the funds needed to develop the new genetic engineering procedures with which the productivity of plants could be *"doubled or even trebled"*.

Under the radar of the mainstream media and public perception the WWF has quietly turned its back on solutions based on supporting smallholder farming structures; on the food sovereignty of nations; and on autonomy.

The WWF is a willing service provider to the giants of the food and energy sectors, supplying industry with a green, progressive image. But ecological indulgences under the banner of the panda have their price: companies pay sizable license fees for using the WWF panda in their advertising and packaging. Big business presumably pays even higher sums to the WWF for studies conducted and consultation services rendered. Then there are the enormous individual donations from companies that collaborate with the WWF, in the RSPO or other capacities. The WWF has an especially close-knit relationship with the energy industry. Its partnerships with Shell and BP go back decades. The two oil giants, both now firmly aboard the bioenergy bandwagon, recently begun financing a WWF study entitled: Responsible Cultivation Areas. With the help of the Ecofys Institute the WWF is currently busy conducting geological surveys to find out which forests in the Southern Hemisphere should be retained – and where there is land that is not being used, or used *"productively"*, which can thus be cleared for industrial plantation operations. The WWF and its partners are using these findings to map the world anew.

To avoid any gaps in communication the two petrochemical multinationals have representatives ensconced in the highest leadership organ of the WWF. John H. Loudon, former CEO of Royal Dutch Shell, for many years sat on the Board of Trustees of WWF International, a position now held by a BP man, Antony Burgmans. The Dutchman is a Non-executive Director of British Petroleum – before that he was Chairman of Unilever.

Corporations that are among the worst environmental polluters on the planet rely on the WWF as an effective marketing instrument – but the WWF can only fulfill this function as long as it maintains a public image as an independent and active nature conservancy organization. Without successful nature conservancy projects the panda brand would lose its value for industry.

In Borneo the WWF is helping, on the one hand, to reforest destroyed rainforest areas. At the same time, however, it is also aiding its agribusiness partners in annihilating new, much larger areas of rainforest in the name of sustainability.

8. A Tango with Monsanto

Once a year the 1001 Club invites its members to the exclusive Panda Ball. One dines and discusses the future of the world in select company. Is the Club just a sentimental relict of the founding era with no significance for current WWF policy, as Rob Soutter tried to convince me in our meeting at WWF headquarters in Gland, Switzerland? If it really is just a harmless group of aging nature-loving aristocrats, why are their gatherings as secretive as the Cosa Nostra? Why do members pay a 25,000-dollar initiation fee? What unseen bonds exist amongst the elite 1001?

I knew that if I could get a look at the secret membership list it would help shed light on these matters. It wasn't easy, but after several months of patient research I finally held two editions of the mystery list in my hand – one from 1978, the other from 1987. Both of them came from the estate of British journalist Kevin Dowling, whose early film about the African misadventures of the WWF was never aired. The two lists can now be found on the Internet.

The cover page of the membership list reads simply: The 1001 Members. Some of the names I was seeing for the first time, but most of them sounded familiar, because they were prominent amongst the world's political and financial elite. They included: billionaire Muslim spiritual leader Karim Aga Khan IV; Fiat boss Giovanni Agnelli; Lord Astor of Hever (president of The Times of London); Henry Ford II; Stephen Bechtel (Bechtel Group, USA);

Title page of the membership list of the club „The 1001"

FIERRO VIÑA, Alfonso	Spain
FIERRO VIÑA, Ignacio	Spain
FINCKENSTEIN, Count Karl-Wilhelm von	Germany
FIRMENICH, Roger	Switzerland
FISCHER, Senator Manfred	Germany
FISCHER, Théodore	Switzerland
FISCHER, Willem A.	Netherlands
FLAMAND, Jean F.	France
FLICK, Dr. Friedrich Karl	Germany
FOCKEMA ANDREAE, W. H.	Netherlands
FOLCH RUSIÑOL, Alberto	Spain
FORD, Benson	U.S.A.
FORD, Henry, II	U.S.A.
FORTE, Lady	United Kingdom
FORTE, Rocco J. V.	United Kingdom
FOURCROY, Jean-Louis	Belgium
FOURCROY, Mrs. Jean-Louis	Belgium
FOX, Mrs. Harry	U.S.A.
FRAGA-IRIBARNE, Ambassador Manuel	Spain
FRALICH, John S.	Canada
FRANCK, Eric	Belgium
FRANCK, Louis	Belgium
FRANKLIN, Cyril M. E.	United Kingdom
FRANTZ, Mrs. Ann	U.S.A.
FRASER, Bt, Sir Hugh	United Kingdom
FREDERIKS, Arthur	Netherlands
FREUDENBERG VON LOEWIS, Harley	Germany
FRICK, Dr. Hans Wolfgang	Switzerland
FRIDRIKSSON, Dr. Sturla	Iceland

Extract of the membership list of the club „The 1001"

Berthold Beitz (Krupp); Martine Cartier-Bresson; Joseph Cullman III (CEO Philip Morris); Charles de Chambrun; H.R.H. Prince Philip, the Duke of Edinburgh; Sir Eric Drake (General Director of British Petroleum); Friedrich

Karl Flick (Germany); Manuel Fraga-Iribarne (Franco's Minister of Information); C. Gerald Goldsmith; Ferdinand H.M. Grapperhaus (Dutch Undersecretary); Max Grundig (Germany); beer baron Alfred Heineken; Lukas Hoffmann (Hoffmann-La Roche); Lord John King (British Airways); Daniel K. Ludwig (USA); Sheikh Salim Bin Laden (elder brother of Osama Bin Laden); John H. Loudon (CEO Shell); Daniel K. Ludwig; Robert McNamara (Vietnam-era US Secretary of Defense); Mærsk Mc-Kinney Møller (shipping magnate); Queen Juliana of the Netherlands; Keshub Mahindra (India); Harry Oppenheimer (Anglo American Corporation); David Rockefeller (Chase Manhattan Bank); Agha Hasan Abedi (President of BCCI Bank); Tibor Rosenbaum (Banque de Crédit International, Geneva); Baron Edmond Adolphe de Rothschild (France); Juan Antonio Samaranch (Spain); Peter von Siemens (Germany); Baron Hans Heinrich Thyssen-Bornemisza (Switzerland); Dr. Joachim Zahn (Daimler Benz).

The 1001 Club membership lists available included a remarkably large share of South Africans. In addition to Anton Rupert, owner of Rothmans International and Cartier, a few dozen other leading lights of the apartheid regime – almost all of them were former or present members of the white-supremacist group Broederbund. The only black African to have found his way into the elite white brotherhood was the Dictator of Zaire, Mobutu Sese Seko.

Most club members were previous or present top dogs in the oil or mining industries, banking or shipping. Conversation at the Panda Ball presumably does not revolve solely around endangered tigers, elephants and songbirds; talk also surely turns to topics such as business prospects in the energy and food sectors. Most club members have directly influenced the political and economic history of their home countries – leaving a large ecological footprint behind in their wake.

Membership Number 572

The name behind the 1001 Club membership number 572, José Martínez de Hoz, is probably unknown to most. Based in Buenos Aires, Martínez de Hoz is an Argentine oligarch with blood on his hands. He owns over a million hectares of land, is a wild game hunter and founding member of the Argentine WWF, which is called Fundación Vida Silvestre Argentina (FVSA).[48] But most Argentines don't think of Martínez de Hoz as an animal lover: his biggest claim to fame is serving as Minister of the Economy during the military dictatorship of Videla.

Unfortunately I was not able to meet José Martínez de Hoz in person, because in the summer of 2010 he had been arrested for crimes against humanity – after twenty years of living unchallenged, escaping justice. At this writing he was under house arrest. His attorney conveyed the message that his client did not wish to accept visitors. There is a photograph of Martínez de Hoz shortly before his arrest: a gaunt old man on his way home with a baker's bag in his hand. Hard to believe that the sensitive-looking geriatric with the friendly smile had been the number two man in a brutal and bloody military dictatorship that had ordered the killing of around 30,000 of its own citizens, most of them man and women in the bloom of youth.

As Minister of the Economy, Martínez de Hoz had concerned himself with the *"modernization"* of the Argentine economy, opening the country to the global market and for foreign investors. He was a man with outstanding international contacts, which his membership in the exclusive WWF club no doubt helped him to cultivate. Even after being confined under house arrest to his luxury residence in the Kavanagh high-rise apartment house Martínez de Hoz was still allowed to pursue his business activities undisturbed. Like all wealthy Argentines, he too had invested a lot of money in soy, the foremost plant-based energy crop in the age of the *"green economy"*. And José Martínez de Hoz is not alone: other top functionaries of the Argentine WWF have also harvested the dubious fruits of Argentina's transformation into a soy republic.

On the flight from Washington D.C. to Buenos Aires we flew over northern Argentina at dawn. From above, the green landscape looked like the region's famous Pampa. In fact, the vast deforested expanses beneath us were industrial soy fields. The 1,500-kilometer flight from Salta in the north to Buenos Aires meant 1,500 kilometers of soy monoculture. A full one half of Argentina's arable land is now covered with the *"green gold"* – genetically modified soy from GMO giant Monsanto. The soy monoculture has spread to neighboring countries Brazil and Paraguay like a galloping cancerous growth.

Biofuel from soy for Europe and the USA is eating away the farmland of the people in the Southern Hemisphere – with the ruthless if indirect support of the WWF. Below us small crop duster planes flew across the seemingly endless fields: they were spraying the Monsanto herbicide Roundup, a substance Monsanto chemists had developed from Agent Orange, the notorious, highly toxic defoliant used by the USA in Vietnam to strip the Viet Cong of their lush forest cover.

The Soy Dictatorship

The huge jacaranda trees on the Plaza San Martin had dropped millions of blossoms. Over the purple petal carpet walked the man we had come to meet: Jorge Rulli, known in Argentina for his relentless opposition to the country's soy policies. He looked up squinting, his hand protecting his eyes from the blazing sun. Rulli scanned the high-rise that housed his former archenemy José Martínez de Hoz.

The battles Jorge Rulli has fought in his life had left their mark: a thick bull's neck, a short crop of unruly snow-white hair covering a massive skull and continuing on uninterrupted to form a bristly beard. His weathered features had dug their way deep into his face; torture had left him blind in one eye. In 1967, while Che Guevara was forming his guerrilla unit in the Bolivian jungle, Jorge Rulli had been arrested in Argentina for the first time and ferociously mistreated in custody. His interrogators wanted to know what his mentor Che Guevara was planning for Argentina. The charismatic revolutionary leader had, in fact, considered returning to Argentina after Bolivia to ignite the fire of social revolution in his homeland. But events took a different turn than planned, with a brutal response from the old oligarchy: in the 1970s military dictators seized power throughout South America. It was the beginning of a dark era.

Jorge Rulli was arrested for a second time and brought to a secret prison where he was held and tortured for a year, during which time his wife and children didn't know whether he was dead or alive. Later he had been sentenced to five years in prison. Yet Jorge Rulli told us he did not wish to exact vengeance on Martínez de Hoz: *"He is one of the key figures responsible for the dictatorship, but it's too late to make him pay for his crimes. Now he's sitting up there, a lonely old man locked up with his wife – that's punishment enough."*

Jorge laughed at his own grim joke and pointed at the glass façade on the opposite side of the square, home to the Argentine branch of Monsanto. According to Jorge Rulli the US-based multinational was now the *"secret government of Argentina"*. He compared it in complete earnest to the military dictatorship: *"The monoculture enforced by Monsanto is just as terrible as the military dictatorship. It is destroying my country down to the very roots. Argentina is now the world's biggest open-air laboratory for genetic engineering."*

In 1996 the Argentine government became the first in South America to revoke the prohibition against genetically modified (GM) crops, and proceeded to permit more than half of the country's farmlands to be transformed into a soy wasteland. Argentina is now the world's largest supplier of soybean oil. The majority of it goes to the refineries that make biodiesel for the European market; the rest goes into feed concentrate for intensive livestock farming in the USA, China and Europe. Argentina's political class wants to use soy to help rapidly industrialize the country and thus pay off national debt. A 35 percent share of the profits from soybean biodiesel flows into government coffers in the form of export duty.

Despite impressive growth figures Rulli did not see the soy model as a success. *"The chemicals are destroying the arable soil, the smallholders are being driven out, food supplies have become scarce and expensive. Argentina can no longer even produce enough meat for its own population. But that doesn't bother the government, because the income from the soy export duty is so high that they can use it to support the subsistence of the hundreds of thousands of Argentines who have fled the countryside for the slums of the cities."*

I wanted to know what position the WWF took on Argentina's genetic agricultural revolution. After all, the massive expansion of soy production had exacted a sacrifice not only of farmland for food crops but vast forest areas as well. According to data from the forestry authorities, since 1914 close to half of Argentina's Chaco Province forest had been chopped down.[49] From 2003 on, the tempo of the destruction had accelerated as the soy industry initiated its great leap forward. Continuous satellite surveillance conducted by the conservationist organization Guyra has shown: in May 2012 the deforestation rate was 710 hectares a day. The Argentine WWF has raised resistance, using a study to make its case for classifying 49 percent of the remaining Chaco as *"especially valuable"* habitat subject to strict protection measures. But that was

Jorge Rulli

not enough to reconcile WWF critic Jorge Rulli with the organization: by defining 49 percent of the forest as *"especially worthy of protection"* the WWF was accepting in principle that the rest would be overrun by agribusiness: *"In Argentina the FVSA (Fundación Vida Silvestre Argentina) is not a nature conservancy organization in a literal sense. It and Monsanto are two arms of the same body. Monsanto created the agricultural model that is now predominant in our country – and the FVSA/WWF Argentina is making every effort to make it socially acceptable. It says: GM soy isn't so bad; it can even be produced 'sustainably.'"*

Sizing me up, Jorge Rulli sensed that I still had my doubts. He suggested I get in touch with the father of the Argentine *"soy miracle"*. *"He doesn't actually give interviews, but as a German your chances with him are pretty good."*

A Patriarch's Dialogue

Dr. Héctor Laurence did, in fact, agree without hesitation to a meeting. Laurence is the godfather of the Argentine model: a long-time player in the soy business, in 2005 he also became president of the IFAMA (Internationalal Food and Agribusiness Association). For many years he had also been the South America representative for two foreign GMO firms: Morgan Seeds and Pioneer, a subsidiary of the chemicals giant DuPont. During the same period, from 1998 to 2008, he was president of the Fundación Vida Silvestre Argentina. In 1988 the FVSA had become an associate member of the WWF.

Dr. Héctor Laurence

I met with Dr. Laurence in his office, which was discreetly decorated in subdued shades of colonial blue. The building was on the upscale Avenida 9 de Julio, one of the best addresses in Buenos Aires. The scion of an English immigrant family, Dr. Laurence was a gentleman from top to toe. Although he and his nemesis Jorge Rulli were almost the same age Héctor Laurence appeared younger. That might have been due to his carefully parted gray-free hair, or to his country club outfit: blue blazer, gray flannel trousers, the pungent smell of a musky deodorant. The steely gaze of his blue eyes and each of his vigorous-yet-controlled gestures clearly communicated that he belonged to the Argentine elite. *"Diplomatic waffle"* was not his thing, said Dr. Laurence. *"You Europeans must be told straight out that you are quite backward in some areas, especially when it comes to modern technologies. You have become the victims of leftwing hysterics who denounce genetic engineering as the work of the devil – instead of listening to science."*

I tried to maintain a neutral expression as I posed the key question of my visit: what did the WWF think about the fact that the soil of Argentina was now drenched with Monsanto's herbicide? Hadn't recent laboratory testing by Argentine pharmacologist Prof. Carrasco determined that Roundup damaged human genetic material? Dr. Laurence furrowed his statesmanlike brow and pondered for a moment before answering in English: *"Those experiments are pseudo-scientific propaganda. If you invite me to drink a glass of Roundup or to smell it for a couple of hours directly – no, I would say, this can hurt me, of course. But on the other hand, like anything if you use a new product – and I don't have any relationship with Monsanto, I want to be very clear on that – if you talk about the risks of technology, in terms of accidents or illnesses, we should then eliminate planes and eliminate cars."*

He looked at me for a few seconds in amusement, waiting to see how I would react to his clever comparison. I held my tongue, so he continued, switching back to Spanish: *"The romantics pine for the old Pampa. That's ridiculous. We soy entrepreneurs are farmers too, when it comes down to it; the land is our most important capital. We care for it and safeguard it. Anyone can invest in soy. We no longer need farmers to have agriculture. That has boosted Argentina's efficiency enormously. The Pampa is experiencing a veritable agricultural revolution."*

Dr. Laurence related with pride how he had founded the National Genetic Technology Commission to familiarize the population with the blessings of this technology. In backward Argentina you had to promote progress a bit, because Monsanto had done *"bad PR work, so that many people thought that genetic engineering would lead to babies being born with fish heads and similar nonsense. We have to help Monsanto to market its products more credibly."*

He had felt personally called upon to *"reconcile"* industry with nature. To this end, in 2003 Dr. Laurence had extended invitations to the Forum of the 100 Million, a round table dedicated to the development of the soy industry. He personally had headed both the delegation of the conservationists and that of the business interests – a dialogue with himself? Dr. Laurence responded to my ironic remark with good humor: *"There were a few other people there as well, including the best scientists in our country. I knew both sides of the coin, so I was the right man to reach a compromise."* The forum agreed to approve the planting in Argentina of 100 million tons of soy and maize crops for energy generation.

I reminded the master of dialogue that the industrial cultivation of genetically engineered crops was eliminating vast areas of forest and conventional farmland. At this, deep worry lines creased Dr. Laurence's forehead – it seemed a struggle was raging between the naturalist and the entrepreneur within him: *"Cut-throat competition is unavoidable in a free-market economy. That's why a few secondary forests had to be sacrificed to achieve our ambitious target of 100 million. But arable land is affected more than forests. Some products have experienced losses: sorghum, livestock farming, sunflowers and wheat."*

For Monsanto the endorsement of the *"new green revolution"* by Fundación Vida Silvestre was heaven sent – after years of fighting for moral support for its genetic interventions into nature. With the backing of an Argentinian bishop, Monsanto had attempted to prompt the Pope to put in a good word for genetic engineering. Nothing doing: the Church remained firm. The WWF was the port of last resort. After all, it too had moral authority in society-at-large – when the WWF talked, people listened. Dr. Laurence summed up with pride: *"With the help of the WWF"* Argentina was now *"a green world power."* The 100 million ton goal was achieved in 2010. But that, said Laurence, was just the beginning: *"We're going to double the target to 200 million."* WWF International, too, he added, had now come out in support of genetic engineering *"thanks to our pioneering work in Argentina".*

At the end of this highly instructive conversation I asked Dr. Laurence what he thought of WWF Argentina founder Dr. Martínez de Hoz: *"I know and value him; a great man who served his nation. He is wrongly under house arrest. Like so many defendants from the era of the military government, he has done nothing wrong, I swear to that."*

Still reeling from the revisionist history lesson, I fired a final shot: would Dr. Laurence succeed Martínez de Hoz as a member of the WWF 1001 Club? I believe I caught a sheepish grin flitting across the tanned face before me: *"I still haven't been asked, but it may happen yet."* With such extensive service to his country it would, of course, be a rude injustice to deny him the ascent to the ranks of WWF nobility.

On the Soy Highway

The next morning I drove to the village of Marcos Paz, west of Buenos Aires. The invincible rebel-with-a-cause Jorge Rulli had created an island of peace and tranquility there. He and his family live in an old farmhouse and have transformed the rest of the land into a Garden of Eden of lush, rambling vegetable patches and flower beds. He used seeds gathered on his travels. In the modern supermarkets, said Jorge Rulli, you could only buy big brand name, imported *"standardized food"*. The old traditional village markets used to have a wide variety of fresh fruits and vegetables: *"It's all over with the variety. The globalization of the food industry has led to a dramatic impoverishment of the human diet."*

We had a long, uncomfortable drive ahead of us, going north on the "soy highway". The temperature rose by the hour as we approached the equator. To the left and right the soy fields stretched across vast desolate areas like huge brown cloths. We made a stop at a village called Tuyutí, where we met the last remaining farmer still at work: breeding polo ponies for export to the rich Gulf States. The other farms lay in ruins.

At last count there were 1,000 *"abandoned"* villages in Argentina. When the majority of farmers sell up for good money to the soy companies, the villagers all end up leaving. 61 percent of the area now covered by soy fields in Argentina used to be pastures where cattle grazed, or farmland with crops of wheat, sorghum, potatoes, maize, sunflowers, rice, barley, beans and cotton. Over 400,000 farmers have already given up on agriculture and migrated to the cities. In Tuyutí the only teacher in the village school had only a dozen children left in her class; it used to be four times that.

At the sight of the dilapidated schoolhouse, rage welled up in Jorge's heart: *"With the decline of the villages the culture of the Pampa has disappeared. People are abandoning the countryside because they have no work here anymore. Those who remain risk being poisoned to death. Roundup is the drug of the Argentine economy."*

We spotted the first crop-duster in the distance. Called a Mosquito, it left a huge toxic cloud trailing behind: Roundup from Monsanto. The poisonous substance drizzled down onto the fields were the still small soy plants

Roundup: brand advertising

fought grasses, herbs and weeds for space. The next day, all the plants were brown and dead, except for the soy. It had survived thanks to a special gene built in to resist the toxic herbicide.

Buyers of Monsanto seed are obliged to purchase the companion herbicide Roundup to go with it. *"This 'package deal',"* says Jorge Rulli, *"makes the farmers dependant on Monsanto. At the end of the day, the Roundup Ready model means total corporate control of agricultural production. Apart from that, Roundup contaminates the ground water and the rivers. Amphibians have died off in our rivers. When they start using that poison even the rats and snakes flee to the cities. We are on the precipice of an ecological collapse, but the WWF tells us, in effect: everything's fine; soy is good; you can plant soy sustainably."*

We continued on our road trip across the green-brown monotony of the soy landscape until we reached the port city of Rosario on the shores of the broad, brown Paraná River. Every day hundreds of transport trucks full of soy arrive from all corners of the country at the harbor. From there the freight is shipped off to Europe – or it lands in one of the new refineries that line the riverbanks. They hungrily swallow up the soybeans and discharge them again in the form of biodiesel. Rosario is the heart that pumps the green oil into the bloodstream of the global economy.

Aided by billions in subventions, the European feed-in obligation for biofuels has created an artificial global biofuel market; by the year 2020, according to the EU directive, 10 percent of the fuel in Europe's vehicles must be plant-based. The USA has a similar provision. Arable land is in short supply in Europe, and thus very costly, so biofuel production has been farmed out to the Southern Hemisphere.

The booming biofuel industry has invested billions and given rise to brand new business alliances: automakers such as VW and Toyota are to be found in new consortiums with energy companies BP and Shell, as well as agribusinesses such as Monsanto, Cargill, ADM and Dreyfus. In the age of the *"green economy"* energy and agribusinesses are fusing. 95 percent of the diesel oil produced in Argentina goes to Europe. The ugly word *"bio-imperialism"* is making the rounds in Latin America, Asia and Africa – wherever vast areas have been devoted to fuel crops. The global north is solving its energy problems at the expense of the global south.

Soy Leftists

In earlier, simpler days Jorge Rulli could blame all the evils of the world on the rightwing oligarchs. Nowadays things are a bit more complicated. After all, the presidents and politicians who have pushed the soy model through in South America have mainly been leftwing: *"Even Lula in Brazil joined in, although genetic engineering was prohibited in his country. Monsanto smuggled the genetically modified seed out of Argentina over the borders to Paraguay, Bolivia and Brazil and gave it away to the farmers in these neighboring countries."*

This was to be expected of Monsanto, said Rulli, but the leftwing governments could have said no. Instead they had played the doorman, ushering Monsanto in: *"After they were defeated, the left could have rebounded by becoming an ecological left; instead, they humbly conformed. The chief ideologists of the soy model weren't reactionaries, they were leftists. 40 years ago they were making homemade bombs, which provided a pretense for the putsch, and now they're the loyal servants of Monsanto. History certainly turns some strange somersaults."*

Gustavo Grobocopatel, for example, is now one of Argentina's biggest soy barons. He used to be a card-carrying Communist and a welcome guest in the Soviet Union. Héctor Huergo was once the chief ideologist of the Trotskyite Party. Nowadays he's editor-in-chief of the agricultural supplement to Argentina's biggest newspaper Clarín and has transformed himself into the ideological mastermind of the soy revolution: *"He used to demand agricultural reform and the expropriation of large estate holders; now he's leading the corporate counterrevolution in the countryside."*

Jorge Rulli still keeps in touch with his old comrade: *"I ran into Héctor at a discussion meeting and asked him if he wasn't ashamed to be transforming Argentina into a new colony whose only role is to supply the powerful countries in the north with biofuel. He laughed at me and said: 'My dear Jorge, you're stuck in a 70s mentality.' I stayed nice and friendly and said: 'Okay, our opinions on the economic model differ, but at least admit that we're losing all our biodiversity.' He grinned at me: 'Biodiversity? That can be recreated in the laboratory.' He's become a cynical champagne socialist who's embedded himself in government and is living there like bee in clover. Sometimes I even wish we* had the military dictatorship back – at least you knew who were the good guys and who were the bad."

In Monsanto's Close Embrace

400 kilometers farther to the west we stopped our rattling Peugeot just outside the small town of Laboulaye, because in the otherwise uninhabited landscape we had come across a human being: Fabricio Castillos. The soy farmer was busy repairing his broken-down crop-spraying vehicle. As it turned out, he was an independent small business owner with 130 hectares of land – and a contract to supply one of the biggest soy companies in Argentina, Gustavo Grobocopatel, which pays the current global market price for the soybeans. The farmer alone carries the production risks: *"When I first started it all worked great. For the first few years Monsanto gave us the seeds for virtually nothing. In the meantime the prices have risen drastically. The herbicide Roundup is really expensive. We have to keep spraying more and more because the weeds have become resistant. This year I used twice as much Roundup as I did five years ago. It doesn't pay anymore."*

I asked a naïve question: why he didn't just switch to conventional soy, which was also still sought after on the global market? The farmer shook his head: *"I'm surrounded by genetically modified soy. It would immediately contaminate my seeds. Besides, Monsanto has already bought up most of the seed companies in Argentina. You have to travel far and wide to find conventional seed."*

The *"green gold"* was driving the farmer into bankruptcy. If soy production proved uneconomic, wouldn't it just do away with itself? The farmer had to laugh: *"Unfortunately not. With my 130 hectares I can no longer make any profit; someone with 500 hectares can still make a living, but at some point you'll need 5,000 hectares. Soon the whole country will belong to just a few investment companies,"* said the last of the Mohicans and started off in his sprayer. Time is money.

From Laboulaye we drove almost 1,000 kilometers northwards without stopping. We saw no intact forest areas along the way, only endless fields of soy and maize monocultures. Where were the *"high value"* forests the WWF claims to have saved through its constructive dialogue with industry? Jorge Rulli didn't know either: *"The forests that have been spared are mainly up in the mountains, so they're of no interest to industrial agriculture. The FVSA/WWF Argentina appears to be satisfied with the existing national parks. What's even worse: they're not really doing anything to stop the destruction of the forests in favor of the soy industry."* As he spoke these words he fished a big stack of paper out of his briefcase: the minutes of the meeting of the Forum of the 100 Million.

"Someone" had passed the minutes on to him. The document proves that the WWF had actively participated in choosing which forest areas would be approved for destruction. At the September 2004 meeting of the Forum WWF representative Juan Rodrigo Walsh reported on the achievements of his working group, the Initiative for Forest Conversion, headed by himself. From the beginning the goal of the Forum had been to transform 5 to 12 mil-

lion hectares into land suitable for the *"sustainable"* production of grain and oil fruit. The minutes of the Forum meeting from Sept. 9th 2004 read: *"Juan Rodrigo Walsh reported on the progress made by the Initiative for Forest Conversion, which he coordinates in Argentina and Paraguay with the support of the WWF via the FVSA (WWF Argentina). He described the methods and steps being taken in this dialogue-led process. He concentrated in his report on the subject of sustainability – on a worldwide scale."*[50]

The sacrifice of the forest apparently posed no problem for Dr. Laurence, head of the FVSA/WWF Argentina at the time. Because, according to him, thanks to the soy fields, the Pampa was *"greener now than before"*. Furthermore, to combat soil erosion many agribusinesses were even leaving untouched green strips between the huge monoculture fields: *"Those are green corridors, which allow animals to move freely over a wide area in search of mating partners. Thus biodiversity is maintained."*

For Dr. Laurence the soy boom is a great boon: *"It is contributing to saving our planet."* Because when cultivating GM soy the fields no longer need to be plowed before the seeds are sown. *"This means"*, according to Dr. Laurence, *"that the greenhouse gas CO_2 stays in the ground and is not released into the atmosphere. A tremendous contribution to climate protection."* The soy industry, with Monsanto leading the way, has in the meantime gone before the United Nations World Climate Council to propose rewarding this type of *"no-till agriculture"* with carbon credits. The UN Climate Council is still hesitant, but the lobbyists are applying pressure, as is, not insignificantly, the WWF.

At the 2009 annual conference of the Round Table for Responsible Soy (RTRS) Jason Clay held the closing address on behalf of the WWF. In it he held out the prospect of a hearty helping of extra profits for the soy industry bigwigs present: no-till agriculture, said Clay, would in future be rewarded with carbon credits: *"The challenge now is to find mechanisms to reward producers who protect forest and soil by allowing them to sell carbon alongside their soy. This is a win-win-win situation. Forest and soil are protected, producers have an additional source of income and retailers and brands can now buy responsible soy as a way to reduce their carbon footprint. Preliminary calculations suggest that producers in forest areas can net more income selling carbon than soy. This fundamentally changes soy and makes it a new kind of commodity."*[51]

Jason Clay is now a frequent and sought-after guest speaker at agribusiness industry conferences. He strokes the psyche of the managers and lends deeper meaning to their fight for market dominance: a partnership with the WWF signifies that your production is sustainable and helps nature and humanity.

In reality, no-till agriculture is highly controversial. Long-term US studies have proven that the method arouses false expectations: abstaining from tilling helps to keep only negligible amounts of carbon gases stored underground.[52] The storage that is accomplished is more than outweighed by the disadvantages of no-till cultivation. In the conventional tilling process the weeds are plowed under, becoming an integral part of the soil flora. In the till-less method, on the other hand, the big chemical herbicide guns are sent in to kill off the weeds. Before the

GM soy is even planted, crop-duster pilots have already flown sorties with heavy doses of Roundup to *"prepare"* the fields: a reversion to the stone age of chemical-based agriculture. The constant shower of chemicals leads to the extinction of life in the soil, making it infertile.

To compensate for the loss of organically produced nutrients in the soil, more and more fertilizer is used, but that creates nitrous oxide. Nobel Prizewinning chemist Paul Crutzen from the Max Planck Institute in Mainz has calculated that the use of fertilizer on soy fields releases three to five times more nitrous oxide (laughing gas) than the World Climate Council originally assumed – a miscalculation with fatal consequences, because nitrous oxide warms the global climate three hundred times more than CO_2 greenhouse gas.

Research by American agricultural scientist Prof. Miguel Altieri has shown that for every liter of biofuel produced, 1.27 liters of fossil fuel is burned: in the development of the fields and for the production and transportation of the soy oil.[53] Ergo, energy generation from plant sources exacerbates the problem with greenhouse gases instead of solving it!

It was time to bid farewell to our friend Jorge Rulli. He wanted to head back to Buenos Aires, where an opposition party had invited him to give evidence at a parliamentary hearing on the Argentine food crisis. He also needed to prepare his weekly radio commentary on government agricultural policy on the station Horizonte Sur. Jorge seemed tired as we said our goodbyes. Perhaps he would rather have been sitting in the sun in his garden of global vegetable delights, but he just couldn't give up the fight: *"Although it's not normal that we old ones are fighting the battles of the younger generation."*

There was no run on the political knowledge of his generation, said the aging warrior, because they're all too busy running after the *"green gold"*. Some village festivals in Argentina no longer chose their beauty queen – now it was a soy queen, the reina de la soja. The gold rush had put his countrymen in a feverish state. Not only that, added Jorge Rulli, the industry had donated millions of GM soy schnitzels to the poor to weaken the political firepower of the opposition: *"Soy is packed with feminine hormones."* Jorge winked with his one seeing eye as he said it, but I'm not entirely sure that his reference to political hormone warfare was just a parting joke.

The farther north we went the bigger the soy fields got. There were no farmers left up there, just big corporate estate owners. Everywhere tree stumps jutted up from the ground. Until recently, the whole region had been forest; big soy companies had cleared it, among them the corporation La Moraleja, in which WWF founder José Martínez de Hoz has a stake. We could make out the forested heights of the Andes foothills in the distance. The soy wasteland stretched right up to where the mountains began. Whenever we drove at night we saw a forest burning somewhere. The slash-and-burn deforestation continued apace.

Pizarro

Driving through the outskirts of the small town Orán we came across a little aero club. A Cessna was just coming in for a landing. We waited until the pilot had peeled himself out of the tight cockpit and then I approached him. His Hungarian-born grandfather had been a fighter pilot on the side of the Germans in the 2nd World War, his father was a traffic report pilot – and Julio Molnar was now a low-flyer over the soy fields, spraying the land with poison.

We wanted to shoot some aerial footage with him to document the advance of the soy front. He hesitated a bit and watched with concern as black storm clouds gathered on the horizon: *"We might just make it."* At wind velocities of about 120 km/h the little Cessna shuttered and jolted alarmingly, but the view from above in the evening light made up for the white-knuckle flight. The soy fields gleamed like gold. We flew over a few narrow corridors of forest that had been left unharmed: the paltry remains of an ecologically valuable forest that used to connect the dry savanna Chaco region in the east with the tropical rainforest in the west – until three years ago.

"There used to be huge jaguar stocks here," the pilot shouted above the wind. They had now disappeared from the region. We flew over the village Pizarro, which was surrounded by soy fields. I decided I'd go the next morning and ask the people down there how they felt about the toxic low-flyers thundering overhead.

When we were safely back on the ground I plucked up my courage and asked the pilot what the many burn scars on his face were from. *"It was an accident. We fly at just three meters above the ground at 200 kilometers an hour. That's very dangerous. A year ago I was flying an insecticide sortie at temperatures of over 40 degrees Celsius. I opened the cabin door a crack so as not to suffocate. The poison seeped through and I lost my orientation. I didn't see the high-voltage power lines until it was too late, and I raced right into them. I managed to crawl out of the burning wreckage just in time. I was lucky; the accident investigators told me that 95 percent of pilots involved in similar accidents don't survive."*

Julio Molnar knows how dangerous his freight is for the people below, and he would like to see the authorities enact no-fly zones in the air space near villages. But measures like that are hard to push through, especially up there in the wild north, far from the seat of the central government, especially when the law is on the side of the powerful anyway: *"They often fill our tanks with what they call a 'cocktail', which is a mixture of a whole bunch of different poisons: herbicide, fungicide, insecticide. That's highly toxic; they're not actually allowed to, but most of them do it anyway, to cut costs."*

During our trip along the scenic soy route we repeatedly heard complaints from local villagers: when the crop-dusters are at work many people suffer coughing attacks, they get skin rashes and experience problems with their vision. Julio Molnar slowly shook his head: *"We don't fly directly over the villages, but the people are still subjected to some of it; it's unavoidable. A single gust of wind can carry the substance more than five kilometers away."*

In the small aircraft hangar hall a wiry man stood waiting for our pilot – it was his flight pupil. Julio Molnar introduced him as a doctor from the region. I'm not allowed to reveal his name, because what he had to tell us could cost him his job: *"I'm seeing more and more villagers who are victims of the crop dusting. The most dan-*

gerous toxin, from a medical perspective, is Glyphosat, the main ingredient of Roundup. The hospitals around here are experiencing many stillbirths and babies born with severe deformities."

Official health department data confirmed a fourfold increase in birth defects in the Chaco soy zone. The number of cancer deaths had also risen significantly. Monsanto continued to claim that Roundup was no more dangerous than conventional herbicides, but no one had verified this assertion – except Monsanto itself.

That changed, however, in 2010, when the US scientific journal 'Chemical Research in Toxicology' published the results of a groundbreaking study by Argentine molecular biologist Prof. Andrés Carrasco. At his Institute of Cell Biology and Neurosciences the professor had conducted laboratory tests with Glyphosat on amphibians. Carrasco was so shocked by his own results that he decided to leave the safe confines of his scientific ivory tower and to make his discoveries available for use as ammunition against Monsanto. I met the feisty man, who was not afraid of a heated debate, at an anti-GMO conference in the Belgian city of Gent. He told me about the comprehensive study he had carried out on amphibians, which are very close to humans in their genomic structure. He had injected the test animals with a very low dose of Glyphosat. The result was spontaneous miscarriages and birth defects. The scientist was alarmed: *"There is most definitely a correlation between the Roundup deployments in the countryside and the rising number of birth defects. I was very concerned, and wrote as much to our president. I know Mrs. Kirchner personally because we were at university together. She didn't even answer. The government is closing its eyes to this ticking time bomb and is conducting no systematic epidemiological surveys whatsoever. They're afraid it would mean the end of the entire soy model."*

Carrasco found himself in the crosshairs of Monsanto and the US embassy in Buenos Aires. According to documents published by Wikileaks, they conducted undercover investigations against him, and sections of the Argentine government along with the national mainstream press began an orchestrated campaign to undermine Carrasco's reputation as a serious scientist. Monsanto proponents were up in arms because Carrasco shed doubt on Argentina's position as a *"green superpower"*; in a conversation with me the former WWF President Dr. Héctor Laurence even berated him as a *"charlatan"*, motivated by ideological issues. Prof. Carrasco laughed when I told him that, but it was obvious that the attacks were really getting to him; it took an enormous amount of energy to defend himself against them. He said that a series of university colleagues had also stabbed him in the back. On the other hand – his eyes lit up at this – *"reality"* was stronger than lies. *"The health crisis in the soy zones is such that even the GMO fanatics can no longer deny it."*

Prof. Andrés Carrasco's scientific theses have given encouragement and a voice to the growing movement of fumigated people all over Latin America. Carrasco also mentored the organization of rural Argentine doctors against fumigation. The worldwide protest movement against GMOs was deeply shocked to hear of the death of the courageous and dedicated scientist. Professor Andrés Carrasco died on May 10th, 2014.

Prof. Andrés Carrasco (RIP 2014)

Back to the soy highway – route five, to be exact. The next day we arrived at a village called General Pizarro. A stop emphatically recommended by long-term FVSA/WWF Argentina president Héctor Laurence. There we would be able to marvel at one of the Argentine WWF's *"great successes"* in nature conservation: the Pizarro National Park. According to Laurence, the WWF had saved this *"high-value forest"* from the greed of the provincial government looking to get in on the soy boom profits: it had *"decommissioned"* a 20,000-hectare nature reserve and sold it to the soy industry. This deal had sparked fierce protest by the inhabitants and attracted the attention of the conservationist heavy-hitters, first Greenpeace, later FVSA/WWF Argentina. The environmentalist organizations sued the provincial governor – and won, if only by half.

As a result of the ruling the government had to buy back a portion of the former nature reserve from the corporations. A grand total of 4,000 hectares were all that was left of the 20,000 hectares originally under protection. The soy industry was permitted to keep the remaining majority share. On our flight over Pizarro National Park the day before it had looked tiny, a thin blue strip nestling up to the mountains in the west, with two green thighs branching off to the left and right. The filet cut in the middle had been torn out for the soy that now grew there: better than nothing! Says the WWF. We went in search of park management.

Pizarro was an oblong village with dusty dirt roads. It hadn't rained for months. The villagers said the deforestation was to blame for that; the climate had changed. Train service to the village had long since been discontinued. Black pigs and goats wandered along the old tracks. The park management had set up its office in the crumbling train station, a little room with a wooden table and a warped bookshelf filled with ring binders – that was it.

Park ranger Soledad Rojas smiled at our astonished expressions: *"Welcome to Argentina! We don't even have a vehicle for patrolling the national park. We have to take a bicycle."* How strange! Hadn't the WWF made a big investment in this model project? The grin on Soledad's face grew even broader: *"The WWF didn't join the protest movement until it was almost over. It was we, the residents of this community, who fought for our forest and won. The WWF jumped on the bandwagon and got money from an international organization for it."* WWF representative Ulises Martínez Ortiz confirmed by email that the WWF had received 167,000 dollars from the Global Environmental Fund to develop a *"management plan"* for Pizarro. The money had been spent *"appropriately"*, mainly on the fees of *"consultants"*. Soledad Rojas was somewhat surprised: *"We've seen none of that here."*

The older villagers told us that WWF founder and dictatorship-era Minister of the Economy José Martínez de Hoz used to come to Pizzaro often to go jaguar hunting. The jaguars had outlived the hunt, but their fate had been sealed by the soy industry. Soledad Rojas and the other rangers had found no trace of a jaguar to date: *"Apparently, they're extinct here now. The national park area is too small – and it's cut off. Jaguars migrate over vast areas, from the Chaco savanna in the east and the Yunga rainforest in the west. They can't do that anymore; they'd have to cross a few hundred kilometers of soy fields to do so."*

We decided to spend another day in the environs of the wondrous national park and booked into the only hotel in the area: the Ruta 5 was a dismal roadside inn for truckers, technicians and migrant laborers who work seasonally on the soy fields. The long corridor was teeming with cockroaches and you had to step over three ancient, putrid-smelling dogs to reach your room. The air was black with mosquitoes; the temperature climbed to over 44 degrees Celsius; the television was broken; in the tiny swimming pool was not a drop of water, just an old discarded garden hose.

The next morning we visited small farmer Moisés Rojas, who keeps a couple of pigs, has small maize fields between the trees and grows tomatoes in a small greenhouse to sell at market in the provincial capital Salta. His pigs live from the fruit of the algarroba (carob) tree – he doesn't need any feed concentrate. *"We're the real ecologists,"* he said, *"we use the forest, but we don't destroy it."* Moisés had lost most of his land. *"My land now belongs to a private company based in Buenos Aires. The state leased it to them, although Argentina recognizes customary law. The forest does belong to the state, but it is not allowed to simply expel those who live on and work it."* The district government had given him substitute land, but it's only half the size of the old area and the soil quality is poor. Many farmers had even ended up selling off the replacement land allocated to them; it wasn't big enough to feed their animals. They were now living in the village, on social welfare.

Moisés' neighbor Carlos Ordoñez came by for a chat. For three years he had been waiting in vain for substitute land. The promised compensation money had not materialized either. In the meantime he had opened a little supermarket in the village just to survive. In his opinion the WWF had not treated the farmers well: *"It cooperates with the big corporations and says: this forest is 'degraded' just because we (the locals) farm it. That's how the WWF supplies the government with the grounds for expelling us from the forest. What's so terrible about using the forest? The wood of the black algarroba tree is one of the hardest and most valuable in the world. It can provide a living if you always only just take a little. The soy industry has bulldozed millions of these trees down and burnt the wood – and the WWF closes both eyes."*

In the meantime a whole group of farmers had gathered around us. Farmer Carlos saw the fateful tale of little

Pizzaro as an allegory of the evils of globalization: "*Soy makes us poor and corporations like Cargill rich. The corporation cultivates soy here, refines the oil and sells it on the global market, and for that we lose our farmland. No worries, says Cargill, and imports wheat from one far-flung place on the planet or another so that we here in Pizarro have bread to eat. This is how the agriculture industry makes people totally dependent on them for food: they want total control. As Monsanto always says: 'We feed the world'. Before that company came here we could feed ourselves.*" Although half of northern Argentina's savanna forest has already been eliminated, another 5 million hectares have been given the green light for clearance.

I asked our host Moisés whether he had experienced any problems from the *"agritoxins"*. He pointed up at the treetops: "*Yes, once a plane flew right over our land spraying herbicide. I got a skin rash and the trees lost their leaves.*" Suddenly there was a commotion behind us. His wife, Francisca Sánchez de Rojas, had come out of the house and now vigorously joined the discussion: "*You forgot to mention the baby I lost. I was in the ninth month of my pregnancy with a little girl. I had to have a Caesarean section – the baby was born dead, with severe deformities. Several doctors examined it. They told me: that could be because of the chemicals; you live in a danger zone. Apparently the herbicide had damaged the genetic material. That's what happened to me.*"

Biodiesel has triggered a new wave of structural violence in many nations on earth. Jean Ziegler, former UN Special Rapporteur on the Right to Food, has called the production of fuel crops on farmland "*A crime against hu-*

Francisca Sánchez de Rojas in front of the soy desert

manity". Plant-based renewable energies produce hunger, poverty and death; and yet the WWF continues to promote them.

In May 2010 WWF biomass expert Martina Fleckenstein made the industry a tempting offer. At the World

Biofuels conference, a global industry gathering held in Seville, Spain, she said that, in the WWF's view, the area devoted to the production of sustainable biomass could be extended worldwide to 450 million hectares – an area the size of the entire European Union.[54] If this vision were to become reality it would mean that a third of all agricultural land on earth would be devoted to the cultivation of biofuel plants – a nightmare scenario for human beings and a sure way of exacerbating hunger in the world. Even long-time allies of the WWF have begun to turn their backs on biofuels. In December 2013 senior management at food giants Unilever and Nestlé wrote a letter to the European Union Energy Commissioner. In it they demanded a drastic reduction in the share of food crops used for the production of biofuel. Only then could hunger and climate change be stopped. Just one percent more biofuel, they wrote in their joint appeal, *"would divert enough food for 34 million people"*.[55]

The WWF is becoming increasingly isolated as a biofuel industry lobby organization; it appears to be deaf to the rising critical clamor. Or perhaps not ... I've been told that since the original German publication of this book in the summer of 2012 the public debate it triggered has also led to discussions at management level within the WWF, and possibly even to small changes in policy. On November 28, 2013 WWF Germany published a brochure entitled: 'Searching for sustainability'. In its analysis of the various sustainability certification models for biofuels even the certificates co-created by the WWF itself get a bad rap: *"The analysis shows that some important issues are poorly represented in the approved standards, including the implementation of social and environmental management systems on the corporate level, handling of invasive species, limitation of the use of hazardous chemicals, waste and water management, restoration of riparian areas and segregation of supply chains in order to offer a non-GMO option. Many standards do not adequately address transparency in public reporting, internal system governance and audit scope and intensity."*[56]

In her presentation of the study, Imke Lübbeke, WWF Senior Renewable Energy Policy Officer in Brussels, calls for the European Commission to improve the standards for renewable energies and comes to the staggering conclusion that: *"Poisoned water and polluted soil is too high a price to pay for a full petrol tank."* A small ray of reason is better than none at all. At least the WWF now wants to toughen the criteria for receiving *"green"* certification. But a decisive jump off the biofuel bandwagon is still nowhere in sight.

9. Redistributing the World

What shouldn't be true can't be true. When I told a WWF staffer I've known for some time that, at an RTRS meeting, the WWF had voted with Monsanto in favor of a certification standard for *"responsible"* GM soy, he accused me of being a *"conspiracy nut"*. Collaboration between the WWF and Monsanto was impossible, not least because in August 2004 the WWF had joined other environmentalist groups as a signatory to the Basel Criteria for Responsible Soy Production, a series of guidelines that categorically rejects genetic engineering. But the panda also has two faces when it comes to GMOs.

I flew to Geneva to interview business consultant Jochen Koester. In a telephone conversation beforehand he had already made the cryptic comment: *"I do feel short-changed by the WWF in the genetic engineering department."* Now I stood outside his company TraceConsult with its magnificent view of Lake Geneva. Although he's a big name business consultant for the soy industry, Koester was adamant that doing business with GM soy was out of the question for him on *"ethical"* grounds. Genetically modified soy was, he said, *"massively damaging for human beings"* and it was *"incomprehensible"* to him that the WWF hadn't prevented the two biggest GM giants in the world from being allowed to join the gathering around the Round Table for Responsible Soy: Monsanto from the USA and Syngenta from Switzerland: *"The result will be that, in the future, 80 to 90 percent of soy certified as 'sustainable' will come from genetically modified seed."*

No one could be sure, he said, what long-term health risks GMOs carried. *"It'll take two to three generations before we know the consequences, but Monsanto can't wait that long. The corporation has invested billions in researching genetic engineering, and now they're hell bent on using it, come what may."* That was *"somehow understandable"* the entrepreneur said. But the fact that the WWF, a *"luxury brand among the nature conservancy organizations"*, had gotten into bed with Monsanto, had *"shocked"* him. He knew whereof he spoke, because he himself had worked on the RTRS: *"When it first got going I was convinced that GM soy would never ever get a sustainability certificate."*

In March 2005 the very first gathering of the Round Table on Responsible Soy (RTRS) was held at a luxury hotel in the Brazilian city of Foz do Iguaçu. Chairwoman of the meeting was Yolanda Kakabadse, former Minister of the Environment in Ecuador, elected President of WWF International in 2010. All the big soy industry players where there, among them the four corporations that control the global soy market: Archer Daniels Midland (ADM), Cargill, Bunge and Louis Dreyfus. Also seated at the table were those who finance the green gold trade: Rabobank from the Netherlands and HSBC Bank. Both financial institutions hold large blocks of shares in the grain corporations.

Major food multinational Unilever is a founding member of the Round Table, as are industrial seed and pesticide producers DuPont, Pioneer and Bayer. Joining them are newcomers to the biomass business: the conventional oil companies, including Shell. With the participation of the WWF the RTRS has succeeded in bringing together all stakeholders in the soy production and distribution chain to collaborate on setting an international standard for *"sustainable"* soy.

In the beginning the companies were afraid that the WWF might call for too many costly environmental restrictions, but it turned out they needn't have worried: experts regard the RTRS-negotiated standards as soft-boiled and non-committal. They allow producers to continue to chop down forests and unleash chemical warfare on the arable land. The guidelines provide protection from the advance of the soy army for only a few *"high-value primary forests"*. But the real clincher of the negotiations, from the industry perspective, was whether or not the WWF would bite the GMO bullet.

The Pact

Jochen Koester had been a part of the Round Table working group on *"principles"*. *"At one of the first meetings someone brought up the subject of GMOs. A representative of the Executive Committee immediately intervened and said: 'You're not allowed to discuss that here'. We were somewhat taken aback by this censorship. The gag order remained in place, but the next day at least a reason for it was given: the RTRS was 'technology neutral' and would not take a position on genetic engineering."*

"Technology neutrality" was the inroad: in 2009, much to the surprise of many, the RTRS admitted two new active members to its ranks – Monsanto and Syngenta, the two biggest genetic engineering companies in the world. As

soon as the GMO duo had sat down at the Round Table the process of defining the standards for sustainable soy gained momentum, and Jochen Koester's fears became reality: in 2010 the RTRS adopted the guidelines for *"responsible soy"* – with the affirmative votes of the WWF and Monsanto.

The statement of the association itself couldn't be more straightforward: *"RTRS is a voluntary certification program developed by The Round Table on Responsible Soy Association. It is applicable to all kinds of soybeans, including conventionally grown, organic, and genetically modified. It has been designed to be used for all scales of soy production and all the countries where soy is produced."*[57]

For the GMO corporations the ratification of these guidelines was a victory from start to finish: a method of production proven risky to humankind and nature had been anointed *"sustainable"* with the stamp of the trusted panda.

Monsanto could now encroach on the rainforest for its soy production in a certified sustainable manner. Previously, soy cultivation in the hot, humid climate of the Amazon River basin had been a losing proposition: the soy plants were attacked and destroyed by fungi, insects and competing plant life. But since receiving the expedient new certification Monsanto has begun flooding the market with GM soy varieties engineered to tolerate the tropical rainforest climate. It's the shape of things to come: *"sustainable"* rainforest destruction. With the RTRS certificate it helped to develop, the WWF has bestowed a princely gift on the pioneers of genetic engineering.

Jochen Koester is still baffled: *"How could they bring a company like Monsanto on board, a corporation that in*

2009 was awarded a 'prize' for being the company with the world's least ethical trading practices?" I played devil's advocate and allowed that the WWF at least had good intentions in a dialogue with Monsanto management aimed at improving the business practices of the corporation. Jochen Koester had to laugh: *"You don't still believe in Santa Claus do you? Embracing a corporation won't make it better."*

The act of getting into bed with Monsanto, metaphorically speaking, shattered a taboo in the environmentalist movement. The betrayal of fundamental principles thus committed by the WWF triggered a wave of criticism. In a letter dated February 9th 2011, for example, the German League for Nature, Animal Protection and Environment (Deutscher Naturschutzring – DNR) remonstrated with WWF management: *"The RTRS is providing artificial life support for an agricultural system that has long since proved a failure ... When the WWF says that GM soy production is perfectly fine, it helps the corporations and unfortunately it's also a stab in the back to many environmental organizations who have spent years raising the alarm about the environmental and health risks of GM soy."*[58]

Many European WWF members also can't quite see what supporting Monsanto has to do with nature conservancy. They explain it by asserting that corporate-friendly Americans at WWF International had quietly taken control of leadership, although they represented only a *"marginal opinion"*. I wrote Jason Clay to request an interview. The Vice President of WWF USA and Chairmen of the international WWF steering committee Market Transformation had, after all, personally orchestrated the big deals with major agribusiness players, including Monsanto. I wanted him to tell me why the WWF went in for such asymmetrical partnerships – and what it gained by them. Jason Clay gave me a friendly reply, agreeing to an interview based on my written questions, submitted beforehand. We made an appointment to meet at his Washington, D.C. office.

Shortly before we were due to meet, Clay's press secretary cancelled: unfortunately Jason Clay would have to distance himself from the interview because WWF Germany had *"some questions and concerns about your TV special ... We are a partnership organization and we need to defer to the German office."* I called WWF Germany spokesman Jörn Ehlers. He was in high spirits, thinking he had scored a little victory: *"I can understand that the cancellation is annoying for you, but it's good for us."* I asked why the German office had applied so much pressure. *"Because if Jason Clay were to get too expansive we could lose sponsors and contributors."*

Many WWF members still believe that sustainability certification for GM soy was just some sort of negotiation slip-up: their *"own people"* had allowed themselves to be hoodwinked by Monsanto. Apparently that kind of thing does happen, but subsequent research would prove that this attempt at an explanation was not founded in reality.

Jason Clay

Monsanto, Cargill, Unilever and Syngenta are the joint founders of a powerful international lobbyist association, the Food & Agriculture Trade Policy Council. Its mission is to spread the gospel of GMOs throughout the world. The council propagates a new *"green revolution"* that would use genetic engineering to overcome famine on earth. The WWF is the only NGO represented in this lobbyist organization – by Jason Clay.

In the summer of 2010, at a Global Harvest Initiative conference in Washington D.C., spokespeople for Monsanto and DuPont took to the stage, beating the drum for the intensive farming of the future. Jason Clay of the WWF was next up to the podium. In his speech he professed unambiguous faith in genetic engineering: *"We need to freeze the footprint of agriculture. We think there are 7 or 8 things – and you can disagree with that, and that's great, let's get the discussion started – that we need to work on to do that. One is genetics. We have got to produce more with less. We've got to focus not just on temperate crops, and not just on annual crops, but on tropical crops, on 'orphan' crops, on crops that produce more calories per input, per hectare, with fewer impacts."*[59]

As an example of the potential of genetic modification Jason Clay referred to a study financed by mega grain wholesaler Cargill. It concluded: with genetic engineering the production of palm oil could be doubled. And: the food supply problems of the world's poorest countries could – according to Jason Clay – only be solved with the help of GMOs, which would enable each tree to deliver a harvest of three times the conventional amount of mangos, cacao beans or bananas. *"We need to get our priorities right: We need to start focusing on the food production: Where it's needed, what's needed, and how to move* *forward. It takes 15 years at least (and maybe longer as we go along), to bring a genetically engineered product to market. If we don't start today, we're already at 2025. The clock is ticking, we need to get moving."*⁶⁰

This message was no doubt music to the ears of Monsanto boss Hugh Grant, as it clearly echoed his mantra: *"We feed the world"*. For Grant, the alliance with the WWF has proved a strategic success. For the first time, an independent, influential civil society entity had said an unreserved "yes" to genetic engineering – no "ifs" or "buts".

Dr. Jason Clay

Jason Clay, who habitually opens his lectures by mentioning that he grew up on a small farm in Missouri, knows how to modulate the key. When addressing an audience of environmentalists or intellectuals instead of big business representatives he pitches his talk accordingly: as an overture he attacks the corporations, criticizing their destructive ecological footprint, a crescendo that culminates in the cathartic trumpet call: when the WWF *"embraces"* the global market players, the evils of the world vanish.

In his July 2010 talk at the TED Global Conference in Edinburgh, Jason Clay even went as far as saying that he would enter partnership agreements with the 100 most important corporations on the planet. According to Clay's data these companies control the extraction, production and the global trade in the world's 15 most significant commodities: *"We've got to take what we've learned in private, voluntary standards, of what the best producers in the world are doing, and use that to inform government regulation, so we can shift the entire performance curve. We can't just identify the best, we've got to move the rest."*[61]

Blackwater

In Washington D.C. I came into contact with a WWF department head. He knew that headquarters had decided I was persona non grata, but he didn't care. Still, I'd rather not mention his name, because he didn't want to be seen within the organization as *"disloyal"*. A conservationist of many years' standing, he no longer felt at home at the WWF. The reins were now in the hands of marketing experts and managers who had come to the WWF from industry: *"The WWF has lost its principles."* In his view, the soy deal with Monsanto represented the lowest ebb in the moral decline of the WWF; for this reason he was prepared to let me in on a juicy detail about the affair with Monsanto.

"In the summer of 2010 the CEO of Monsanto, Hugh Grant, paid a top-secret visit to WWF USA headquarters in Washington D.C." My informant and most other members of WWF management had not been privy to what was being negotiated behind closed doors. In parting,

the WWF man handed me a copy of an article from the political news weekly 'The Nation': *"So you'll understand why I'm afraid of Jason's new friends."* Back at the hotel I read the article. Although I was well aware that Monsanto was no cheery charity shop, I was still shocked at the content of journalist Jeremy Scahill's exposé. His research revealed that in 2008 Monsanto had hired the infamous private security company Blackwater to infiltrate groups opposing genetic engineering. Typically, the US firm Blackwater would lease mercenary unites to foreign governments for deployment in international and civil wars. Blackwater also carried out special operations for the US Army and the CIA when it was desired that the hand of the US Government remain invisible – especially those involving targeted killings in the name of the *"war on terror"*.

For the Monsanto contract Blackwater deployed its subsidiary Total Intelligence Solutions. According to 'The Nation', in January 2008 TIS boss Cofer Black met up in Zurich with Monsanto's head of security Kevin Wilson. At that meeting Blackwater advised Monsanto to create its own intelligence department. This private corporate secret service agency should then plant its agents in anti-GMO groups and media to subvert them from within.[62] Greetings from Big Brother.

Monsanto has used its tight grasp on the seed for the most significant agricultural commodities to conquer entire national economies, and could one day control entire nations. The prospect of Monsanto's "brave new world" is horrifying for virtually everyone – except, that is, for the WWF.

The Friends of Europe

The European WWF organizations fear a mass membership exodus if it becomes known how close the embrace between their organization and Monsanto has become. In response to the original German publication of this book in 2012 WWF Germany set up a *"fact check"* website as a forum for concerned members and donors. There the organization was at first disingenuous in the matter of its controversial partner, claiming: *"The WWF does not cooperate with Monsanto."* Furthermore, they claimed to have never received money from the corporation. Only a few days later, however, the WWF had to retract the claim and admit that WWF USA had, in fact, accepted donations from Monsanto between 1985 and 1992 – to the tune of 103,000 dollars.[63]

Even confirmed WWF supporters are no longer convinced by the organization's attempts at self-defense. In an entry from June 28th 2011, a contributor to the WWF Germany online forum summed up his subjective assessment: *"So the impression remains ... that you allow yourselves to be instrumentalized by industry, indeed by the most mafia-like, problematical industry of our times, after weapons and oil."*

The response from WWF management from the same day reads like a confession: *"The fact that we engage in exchanges with certain companies doesn't mean that we have any fondness for these companies at all. Admittedly: sometimes it's incredibly difficult to overcome our own reticence ... but we have only one goal: to prompt companies like Monsanto to change their behavior. That may sound naïve to you, but that's how we think!"*

In an internal document from February 17th 2009, management at WWF International had already looked at possible ways of subverting the pending criticism of its alliance with Monsanto. The paper, destined for the eyes of WWF functionaries only, makes clear that the organization was seeking to reposition itself in the public arena and to renege on previously ratified resolutions: *"WWF needs to develop an updated position on GMOs that, among other things, addresses circumstances where GM production is already widespread."*[64]

In regard to stemming opposition within the rank and file, it reads: *"WWF needs to proactively manage the potential risk to its reputation and membership base due to perceptions that it is promoting GM companies or that the RTRS is a pro-GM process."* The paper proposes an immediate intervention: *"WWF Switzerland will explore options for the registered address of the RTRS to be changed."* This was relevant because, to date, the Round Table for Responsible Soy, at which Monsanto and the WWF sit side-by-side, had been headquartered at Hohlstrasse 110 in Zurich; WWF Switzerland happened to share the same address. Would such cosmetic maneuvers really placate their own membership base?

I discovered another document along the way: the program from a WWF International training course for corporate managers. The content makes amply clear that the WWF cooperation with Monsanto is not an exclusively American affair. Entitled: 'Step forward to be a ONE PLANET LEADER – the applied sustainability programme for business leaders and executives', the WWF executive training course would, among other things, teach managers how to convert their companies to *"sustainable business models"*, with no losses to the bottom line. On the contrary: the established trend in the age of climate change was that a green image sent profits skyrocketing.

Participants paid the handsome fee of almost 13,000 dollars for the course, which was held over several days in idyllic Swiss Ittingen, in the exclusive ambiance of a former monastery. Seminar guests were fed only *"organically farmed vegetables"* – perhaps the ultimate punishment for some of the executives on the course. The list of participants reveals that many global corporations have already sent their managers to the WWF Swiss greenwashing academy: ABN Amro, Canon, Coca-Cola, Dow, Johnson & Johnson, Nestlé, Nokia, Shell and – Monsanto.

In Brussels I asked Nina Holland of the European Corporate Observatory about this. The watchdog organization she works for focuses on big corporations predisposed to lobbyism, so the WWF was also on Nina Holland's radar. The WWF European Policy Office in Brussels is located on the upscale Avenue de Tervurenlaan, only about 100 meters away from the Europe representation of Monsanto.

According to Nina Holland the some 30 WWF staffers knocking on doors in Brussels have direct access to EU Commissioners and to the powerful General Directors for Agriculture, Environment and Transport. They were welcome guests with a reputation for being *"constructive"*. The WWF is invariably invited to conferences and seminars on climate policy, energy, water and also transportation, often as the only environmental organization among industrialists. Many of these high-level meetings are private events, planned and financed by industry associations or individual corporations. The WWF is also the only nature conservancy organization to enjoy membership in the Friends of Europe, one of the most influential think tanks in Brussels.

Nina Holland assessed the WWF as a lobbying force to be reckoned with in the Brussels corridors of power. Since 2004 she had observed the organization promoting plant-based fuels, pushing in particular for the approval of fuel from GM soy: *"The corporations took no interest in the Basel Criteria – a sustainability standard that expressly forbade genetic engineering. The WWF was also a signatory to the Basel Criteria. But the ink on its signature had barely dried when it got together with the industry to hatch an alternative proposal, the Round Table for Responsible Soy. The goal, it seems to me, and from the very beginning, was to gain entry for GM soy to the European renewable energies market. The people from the Brussels WWF office met with the relevant EU officials and lobbied them for EU accreditation of the private RTRS certification system."*

Together we reviewed the staff list of the WWF European Policy office in Brussels. Not an American among them; the entire staff came from European WWF organizations. Heading the WWF EU crew was Imke Lübbeke from WWF Germany. She is Senior European Policy Officer for Bioenergy. For Nina Holland this was clear evidence that European WWF representatives don't always tell their members the truth: *"The Americans are not major stakeholders in the RTRS certification for soy. It was a project for Europe from the very start. Without the WWF, Monsanto would never have been able to gain entry to Eu-*

rope so quickly and easily. And I'm afraid that's only the first step. In two years at the latest we'll be hearing: if Monsanto plants can be farmed responsibly and sustainably in Latin America, then why not in Europe?"

On July 19th 2011, the European Union ruled to grant accreditation to the RTRS certification seal. That put biodiesel from GM soy in the category of *"renewable energy from sustainable agriculture"*. Just a short time later the first shipload of RTRS soy arrived in Rotterdam. It came from the company Amaggi, the biggest soy producer in Brazil and a partner of the WWF at the Round Table for Responsible Soy.

Until 2007 one of the owners of the Grupo Amaggi, Blairo Maggi, was governor of the soy province Mato Grosso and has the dubious reputation of being Brazil's biggest deforester. 40 percent of all forest clearance in Brazil can be attributed to his company. A fact that doesn't bother Maggi in the least: *"That 40 percent means nothing at all to me. I don't feel the slightest bit guilty. We still have an area of virgin forest bigger than Europe, so there's nothing to be worried about."*[65]

Eating Ice Cream for the Rainforest

Jason Clay personifies like no other WWF policy for the 21st century. He advocates cozying up to big business far more openly and radically than his Old World colleagues. Who is this Jason Clay, who wants to link arms with Monsanto to save the planet? What motivates him and what does he really believe?

Old friends and associates recall that in the late 1970s and 1980s he was an enthusiastic young anthropologist working with the indigenous rights organization Cultural Survival. He was in charge of editing the Cultural Survival Quarterly, an important and influential journal that gave support to indigenous peoples fighting for their autonomy. Clay was not a field anthropologist; he never spent much time in the field with indigenous peoples, but he spoke eloquently in defense of their rights, invariably backing up his talks with a briefcase full of statistics. In 1988, Clay wrote: *"The people that have used tropical forests for centuries without destroying them are now, in turn, being destroyed ... Western attitudes, which stress the conquering of nature, have had disastrous consequences ..."*[66]

Today, Clay is a different person altogether. Once thin as a rail, he has put on considerable weight and has adopted the manner and inflection of the multinational managers he now calls his partners. He is a powerful figure within WWF International, and while there is opposition to his views and approach within his own organization, there are few who would challenge him openly. I wanted to know how the great WWF strategist ticked, but as I'd been forbidden from speaking with him, I had to make a detour to Colorado to find out.

Anthropologist Mac Chapin makes his home these days at the foot of the Rocky Mountains, just north of the town of Boulder. He had worked closely with Jason Clay at Cultural Survival from 1987 through 1993: *"During the first years, Jason was a very responsible professional. He was adept at putting together the issues of the Quarterly – a daunting task that involved eliciting articles from knowl-*

edgeable scholars who were working with endangered indigenous peoples around the world, all done on a tight schedule. Yet as time passed, he grew bored with the journal and set off in a new direction: the marketing of rainforest products. In 1989, he founded Cultural Survival Enterprises, which was set up to bring indigenous peoples into the international market. One of the

Mac Chapin

most visible results of this was the development of Rainforest Crunch, a caramel and nut candy that was also turned into a line of ice cream sold by the popular Ben & Jerry's Ice Cream brand. The nuts – mainly cashews and Brazil nuts – were supposedly hand-harvested by indigenous peoples living in the rainforest." Chapin laughed. "Virtually none of the ingredients were actually produced by indigenous peoples." The sugar came from industrial plantations and the milk came from cows, and both were produced on land that was decidedly not covered with rainforest. Beyond this, the aluminum packaging for Rainforest Crunch candy was hardly a *"sustainable"* product. *"It was all a bluff, but it worked. Ben & Jerry's Rainforest Crunch was a tremendous success."* The message on the package was: *"Rainforest Crunch shows us that the rainforest is more profitable when its nuts, fruits, and medicinal plants are traditionally cultivated and harvested than when its trees are felled for a quick profit."*

A few years after the launch of Jason Clay's marketing idea inquisitive journalists from The Boston Globe uncovered the truth: Five percent of the nuts at most came from a cooperative in the rainforest; Ben & Jerry's bought the bulk of their nuts wholesale from non-indigenous middlemen. Not only that: in order to get what they needed, it turned out that the company could not count on indigenous producers, for the quality of nut they produced was uneven and they could not supply enough of them. In the end, the nut-gatherers were not Indios but rather mestizo farmers in non-indigenous regions, and most of the nuts came from areas that were not rainforest.[67]

In the face of this PR disaster, Ben & Jerry's pulled the emergency brake and in 1994 removed the flavor from their inventory. It had all been a success nonetheless, claimed the company, because Rainforest Crunch had at least *"created demand for rainforest products"*.

"This was hardly a success," says Chapin. Instead of empowering indigenous peoples, it was undercutting them. Rainforest Crunch would be widely remembered as a marketing fraud. Within the WWF, however, it became a model for future campaigns that coax money out of donors' pockets while simultaneously easing their conscience. Do you want to save the African savannah? Just chug down some Krombacher beer or jet around the world with LTU. Are you serious about saving the polar bear from extinction? Just drink more Coca-Cola. One has to ask: Is the WWF really concerned about the climate or just with the cash?

Chapin has followed the metamorphosis of his former colleague with apprehension. *"Jason found marketing sexy, and it gave him an opportunity to deal with large companies. When he went to work with WWF in the mid-1990s, he rapidly rose to the top. He fit the bill, for WWF and the other large conservation organizations, all of them growing rapidly in size, were anxious to bring in more money, and marketing on the scale Jason promoted was in line with this goal. He is a smooth power broker and very ambitious, and he intimidates many of the traditional conservationists in the organization."*

For years, Chapin and his colleagues worked closely with WWF personnel, trying to bring them together with indigenous groups to forge alliances. In his experience, conservationists working in the field often do a good job; they deal evenly and respectfully with the people living in the forests they want to protect. Yet the main office has a different approach: they are after money, and that is where the conflict is. I read him Jason Clay's statement about *"embracing"* the 100 biggest corporations in the world to *"improve"* them. Chapin cracked a smile: *"These large corporations are very powerful. They are like sharks and WWF is like a pilot fish that swims alongside, picking up scraps left by the predator. The WWF pilot fish is simply pretending to direct the corporate shark in this direction or that. No small organization like WWF is going to influence a multinational company like Chevron-Texaco or Monsanto. All the companies are looking for is a green fig leaf, and that is what WWF supplies – for money, of course."*

Chapin is at peace living in the Rockies. He is semi-retired, an adjunct professor at the nearby University of

Colorado, and he continues working with indigenous peoples in the field. Yet he is not sanguine about the prospects of success. *"There are simply too many forces moving against indigenous peoples these days. Petroleum companies began drilling in tropical rainforests on a large scale in the 1980s; mining operations have arrived, and now rainforest is being cleared for oil palm, sugar cane, and soy for the production of biofuels. Forest is being cleared at an ever-accelerating rate, and there is seemingly no way to stop it. Now that we have the large conservation organizations working closely with corporations that include oil companies such as Chevron-Texaco and Mobile, they have come to work against the interests of indigenous peoples. This is a very alarming trend."*

If I wanted to understand the WWF, said Chapin, I should follow the money. The WWF, along with the other big nature advocacy groups such as Conservation International and The Nature Conservancy, has become financially dependent on Big Industry. *"It is ironic that the large conservation organizations are working hand-in-glove with companies that are destroying the ecosystems that they claim to be protecting. On the other side of the equation, there is little evidence that WWF's approach will help indigenous peoples in their struggles to save the rainforest. In the late 1980s the indigenous groups of the Amazon Basin proposed an alliance with the conservationists, and WWF produced a position paper that spoke of working together. But nothing came of it."*

Chapin is an affable man who generally avoids conflict. Yet in 2004 he drew the ire of the conservationists by publishing a polemic piece titled "A Challenge to Con-

servationists" in World Watch Magazine. In this article, he made it public that the Ford Foundation, which has over the years funded many WWF programs, was conducting a critical evaluation of relations between indigenous peoples and the large conservation organizations. *"A number of indigenous organizations had complained to Ford that the conservationists were being abusive,"* says Chapin. *"Ford hired two consultants who were looking into the matter, and what they were finding was alarming."*

According to Chapin, in most cases the conservationists were riding roughshod over the peoples living in rainforest areas they claimed to be protecting. Despite claiming that they were partnering with indigenous peoples, they were instead partnering with the corporations that were displacing the indigenous peoples. WWF and the other conservation groups were silent on their arrangements with the companies. They said they were *"apolitical"* and did not on principle take sides in conflicts; yet this was exactly what they were doing. The Ford Foundation put a gag order on the evaluation. Leading the charge was Yolanda Kakabadse, then-President of the International Union for the Conservation of Nature (IUCN). Since January 2010 she has been President of WWF International.

Chapin fears that the tropical ecosystems of much of Latin America, the homes of many vulnerable indigenous peoples, will be destroyed within the coming decades. This is happening in the Amazon Basin. Extractive corporations from all over the world *"are running amok, and the conservationists find themselves hog-tied with the financial arrangements they have with the corporations. The last thing they want to do is partner with indigenous peoples.*

In this context, the large conservation organizations have become henchmen of the corporations; and with personnel like Jason Clay, they are adopting their values."

The Insider

There was still a place in his heart for the WWF: *"I had a lot of freedom in carrying out my projects. It's not all bad, what the WWF does!"*

John sat across from me in a little café in Brussels. John is not his real name, but he'd like to remain anonymous. He's afraid of the long arm of the WWF should he decide to apply for a job with another NGO. John had been responsible for international WWF projects but had since left the organization: *"My problem with the WWF is its dialogue policy, which has been adopted worldwide. They disappear behind closed doors to negotiate with the powerful and they think they'll make the world a better place that way. Unfortunately I don't know of a single example where that has worked. The only thing that has ever brought success is when people unite in resistance and together make something happen. Just think of Germany: you don't have dialogue to thank for the nuclear power phase-out; it's down to the anti-nuclear movement that persevered for decades. To win in a conflict you have to persevere. The WWF isn't capable of confrontation; it's enough to satisfy senior members when the WWF gets more press than Greenpeace."*

John had belonged to the enthusiastic midsection of the WWF structure; in his opinion, many round tables with industry partners are a total sham that do nothing for nature. The round table for dams had been the last straw for John: *"The WWF attitude is: we can't stop them building mega-dams in the rainforests of Africa and Latin America anyway, so we'll just concentrate on 'better practice' instead, in other words: you can't prevent something bad, only make it better."*

I argued that hydraulic power was, at least, better than cultivating crops for fuel, because it's cleaner and whole forests aren't cleared to produce it. John rejected this argument: *"Palm oil plantations and soy monoculture are situated on the peripheries of the rainforests, but the dams are built bang in the middle of the world's most valuable rainforests. They destroy the rainforest starting right from the heart of it. 80 dams are now in planning for along the Amazon alone. To build the dams, huge swaths are cut through the forests for roads and for the power lines above. Thousands of migrant workers come from other parts of the country to work on the building site and then they burn down the forest so they can settle and farm there. The Indios call them 'carnivores', and with them comes alcohol, degradation and the swift trade in prostitution. Although the WWF knows that the giant dams destroy both nature and indigenous cultures it has reconciled itself to their proliferation."*

John had fought in vain against the WWF's change of course: *"The WWF, along with other big NGOs, gives climate change priority over everything else, which blinds them to the new problems that are actually created by the so-called 'renewable industries'. What's even worse is the fact that the WWF has actually helped industry lower the ecological standards for dam construction."* The old standards, which had been developed jointly by the World Commission on Dams and the World Bank, were a solid set of environmental regulations, but far too stringent for the taste of the big property developers.

So the International Hydropower Association (IHA) had initiated a round table where partners would gather for a 'dialogue' that would bring forth new, lower standards. *"The WWF accepted the offer and sat down together with industry at the negotiation table. The result was presented in the summer of 2011, and it was clearly a change for the worse. The standards are not binding; compliance with them is dependant on the good will of the companies involved."*

I found the result of the dialogue on the International Hydropower Association (IHA) website: the Hydropower Sustainability Assessment Protocol. Signatories to the protocol include major energy companies, as well as banks and government agencies, and two lone non-profits: the WWF and the US organization Nature Conservancy. The protocol consists of non-binding recommendations that had been reached *"by consensus"*. A typical example of the elastic language used: *"Criteria or principles for analysis of alternatives might include, by way of example, siting on tributary stream rather than mainstream rivers; avoidance of high value biodiversity areas; avoidance of resettlement."*[68]

According to my contact John, on this occasion the WWF had bestowed the use of its good name upon industry without any tangible quid pro quo: *"It's a typical negotiation trap. You spend months trying to come up with the right phrasing and then sign up to a protocol that seems promising, but actually has no significance in practice. Suddenly you find yourself sitting in the same boat with industry. The chief negotiators of NGOs often experience that as recognition of a sort – it's a psychological phenomenon. Then an external voice comes along and criticizes the agreement, which they take as a personal attack, having participated in the deal. So then they defend it as an important step forward."*

John was convinced that in signing up to this protocol, the WWF had bowed out of the fight against the mega-dams for good: *"In practice, no one pays any attention to the agreed standards. In my opinion, the dialogue strategy of the WWF is helping to destroy the natural environment, because the companies now have free rein to embark on a huge business venture – there are 1,500 dams in planning worldwide. The 'green economy' will accelerate the destruction of the planet."*

The Southern Hemisphere, especially Africa, provides a tempting prospect of mega-profits from hydropower. The Grand Inga Dam being planned for the Democratic Republic of Congo will be the world's largest. Speaking of these developments over coffee in the old town of Brussels John suddenly seemed tired and discouraged. Was he? *"It has become harder to fight. Globalization makes you helpless. You often don't know your enemy anymore, and the local indigenous people are left to cope alone; most of us in the West have turned our backs on the culture of resistance. Even within the WWF I was considered a radical because of my views."*

As radical as blockbuster film director James Cameron, who in 2010, together with Bill Clinton, headed out to Brazil to offer support to the Indios in their fight against the mega hydroelectric dam complex Belo Monte. 20,000 indigenous people had been earmarked for resettlement because of the project, and a further 20,000 would be forced out because the dam would destroy their fish reserves – 'Avatar' on earth. John recalled Cameron's encounter with the Indios: *"He felt like he was in a scene from his own film, except that the blue-skinned Na'vi natives of his fictional Pandora where now a real, red-skinned people called Kayapó. Like the Na'vi they fought with bow and arrow against an enemy fully equipped with high-tech gear."*

In Cameron's film the Na'vi are victorious; the indigenous people of Brazil's Xingu River basin, on the other hand, appear to have lost the fight. Disregarding the protests, in August 2011, the Brazilian government issued a building permit. One of the tribal chiefs wept when the decision was made public; others were not about to give up the fight: *"They were very determined, and told me that when the bulldozers came they would reach for their weapons and there would be war. I think they still have no idea of what's actually coming their way."*

WWF Superpower

WWF studies show that currently about 30 percent of the earth's surface is still covered by more or less untouched natural environments, in which mainly indigenous peoples live. It appears the WWF has entered into discreet dealings with the giants of the energy and agricultural sectors, with the aim of saving some of these remaining biotopes. The organization finds itself in a dilemma: it can't stop the forward march of intensive plantation farming in Africa, Asia and Latin America, yet urges that at least 10 percent of the planet's surface area remain untouched under stringent protection measures. Some WWF staffers have even recently begun speaking of 20 percent. Industrial players on the other hand, choose to interpret the WWF demands to suit themselves: if just 10 percent has to be saved, that means the rest of all natural environments are fair game for the last raid of the energy and agriculture companies. In the Southern Hemisphere there are still huge forest areas and savannas that haven't yet been made into national parks. According to the WWF's surface area arithmetic, more than half of the land in Indonesia, Brazil and Argentina is still *"unused"*, in Papua it's even 90 percent. Global agribusiness wants this land, and the WWF is doing nothing to stop it.

As a moral justification for their broad capitulation to agribusiness, the WWF and others resort to an apocalyptical scenario: if more land is not freed up for food and bioenergy crops, in 2050 there will be wars over land, food and water. When the planet is home to nine billion people, agricultural production will have to be double what it is now. But this alarming projection quickly collapses when you consider the fact that currently, half of all food produced spoils or is thrown away before it ever reaches the consumer. The WWF calculation also gives far too little consideration to the risks of globalized industrial agriculture based on genetic engineering and monocultures. The way of Monsanto and its partners is only one option, but by no means the only one.

For years now, the agricultural experts of global development policy organizations and the United Nations have repeatedly called for the support of local smallholder farming. This was the better way to produce enough healthy food, they agreed, and would remain so in the future. Personally, I am convinced that their arguments are better than those of Monsanto and the WWF, yet they continue to lose ground nonetheless. Agribusiness is powerful, well connected in a global network, and can afford to pay its lobbyists and appraisers handsomely. It doesn't waste its breath on long discussions, and before you can turn around, it has already set up shop.

The big players in the global agricultural and energy business are busy buying up land throughout the world. The WWF lends a civilizing veneer to this corporate land grab. The industry round tables are an especially useful tool here: the certification they confer for *"sustainable and socially responsible"* production of *"strategic commodities"* – sugar, wood, biofuels, meat, fish, maize, soy and palm oil – amounts to little more than greenwashing. The certification business is booming – and it's a nice little earner for the WWF.

The WWF straddles the fence: on one side it protects the forest, and on the other it helps corporations lay claim to land not previously in their grasp – land on which people were already living and working. These local people are often a spanner thrown in the works of big business, and thus are forced out. The WWF helps sell the idea of voluntary resettlement to the indigenous peoples with slogans like *"opportunities for a better life"*. When *"the natives"* are won over they are resettled in reservations or the buffer zones of national parks in settlements that resemble human zoos. The previously self-sufficient peoples become dependant on ecotourism and lose their hereditary right to live off the fruits of the forest. That is the cost of survival in the WWF's brave new *"sustainable"* world.

The WWF plays its part in the global system of control that aims to implement a new world order. The organization collaborates with key agribusiness lobbyists and receives millions in funding for its certification systems: from national government budgets, the European Union, the World Bank, and even UN organizations. The WWF has become a political power. This is a result of the fact that during the 1990s Western governments handed over a large part of the bothersome task of nature conservation and environmental policy-making to non-governmental organizations. This privatization of sovereign duties created a vacuum of global proportions, which multinational corporations and a few NGOs have stepped in to fill.

A few dozen individuals who were never elected for the job are busy doing backroom deals that result in global policy decisions in the interest of their industry masters. Nothing less is at stake in these dealings than the distribution of the last exploitable land masses on earth. The protagonists of the global *"green economy"* have detached themselves from national governmental institutions. Decision-making processes are dominated by a few multinational mega-corporations that have wrapped their tentacles around the planet like octopuses. Their senior management is everywhere: on site in the rainforests and on the international committees where key strategic decisions are made. They move a lot more quickly than governments and international political commissions. It's not often that we get to catch a glimpse of the internal structures of this parallel world power; in general, only when an elected politician gets suspicious and starts *"making trouble"*. In 1997, Guy Lutgen, Minister of Agriculture and the Environment in the Walloon Region of Belgium did just that, after the World Bank announced that it had formed a *"forest alliance"* with the WWF.

Via indirect channels, I came into possession of a highly informative correspondence between Guy Lutgen and the President of the World Bank at the time, James D. Wolfensohn. In a less-than-diplomatic letter from 1997 Lutgen warned of the alliance with the WWF. Back then the WWF was calling for at least 10 percent of the forests to be protected by conservation regulations. Lutgen did not want the World Bank to adopt this number. And he did not want private companies, hand-in-hand with the WWF, to be able to issue sustainability certification to themselves. *"In what way is certification 'independent' if its rules have been drawn up by a handful of NGOs working with a few economic groups in the absence of monitoring by official organisations? ... Furthermore there is a risk that certain governments or companies would legitimize non-sustainable practices across 90 % of their forests by bringing 10 % of their less workable forests under protection."*[69]

The Belgian minister's apprehension would prove justified. The sustainability certificates launched on the market by agribusiness and the WWF aren't worth the paper they're written on. Any shopper at a home improvement center can vouch for that: the FSC sustainability label is appearing on more and more wood products and furniture. Most people buy the certified wood in the belief they are doing something good for the rainforest. But do they also read the small print? In most cases, right next to the FSC logo is the harmless-sounding word *"mix"*. But according to the rules of the Forest Stewardship Council, or FSC, that little word means that only 10 percent of the wood thus labeled must come from certified production. The rest may be from industrial tree plantations or recycled material. According to FSC principles, wood from illegal or unverifiable sources or overfelling is excluded. However, customers are offered no means of identifying the exact origins of the certified woods, so traceability is a non-starter.

In reply to his red-flag letter to the World Bank, the foresightful government minister Guy Lutgen received a friendly, non-committal missive from bank president Wolfensohn. He rejected the criticism and affirmed the strategic alliance with the WWF. His answer also managed to casually confirm that there was, in fact, a secret WWF plan, which foresaw the conservation of only 10 percent of the forests: *"With regard to the WWF's minimum 10 % target for forest protected areas, we agree that priorities need to be set and close attention paid to determining adequate percentages for forest cover protection."*[70]

In his letter Wolfensohn insisted that the certification systems be established and administered privately, and not by public authorities. After all, one important aim of certification was to kick-start the trade in tropical woods: *"It may actually help avoid the imposition of trade barriers."* That is the crux of the matter: the WWF alliances and the certification systems they produce are first and foremost about asserting the financial interests of private industry.

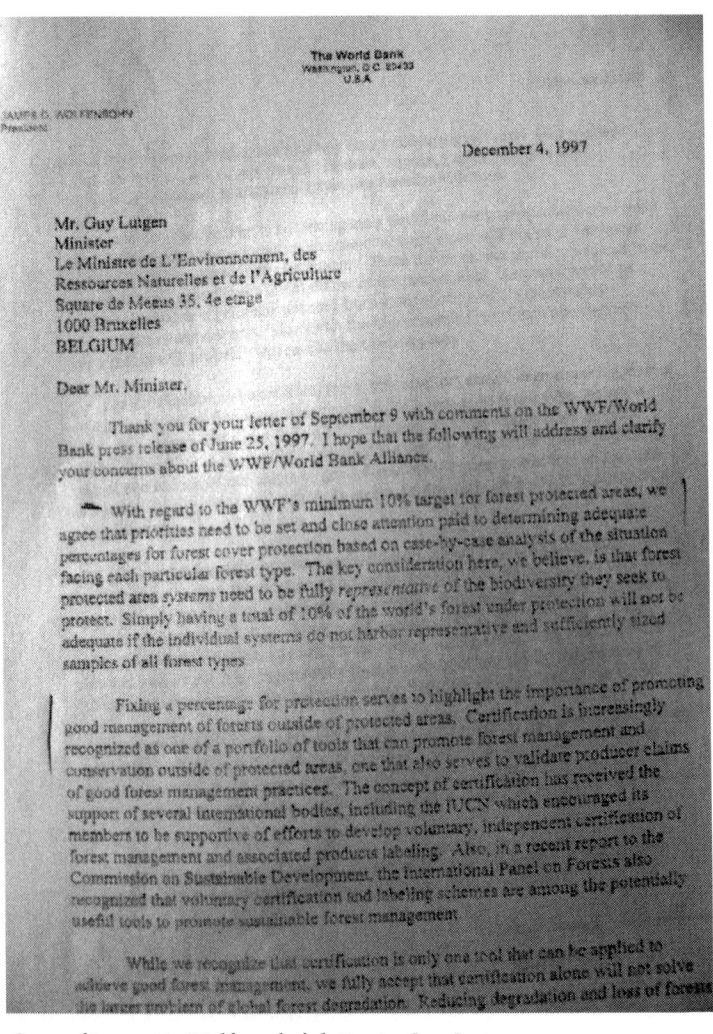

Copy of James D. Wolfensohn's letter to Guy Lutgen

Guy Lutgen wanted to inhibit the power of the WWF because he believed it to have no legitimation whatsoever: *"It appears surprising that an international organization such as the World Bank is entering into an agreement with a non-governmental organization operating as a pressure group without democratic control on action such as certification which hitherto has not been the subject of approval by international bodies."*

The concerns expressed in 1997 by the Belgian government representative fell on deaf ears. For the WWF, the alliance with the rich and powerful World Bank proved to be a brilliant coup. Since 1997 the World Bank and the WWF have often appeared in tandem wherever talk turns to the fate of the world's rainforests, be it in Sumatra, the Amazon, Papua or the Republic of Congo. When the power couple arrives to negotiate with the national government concerned, they usually come bearing a joint master plan for *"sustainable forest management"*. They have the money and the might to enforce their strategy. When the World Bank/WWF has done its job in the vanguard, the modern conquistadores follow: energy and agriculture corporations then sweep in to do the dirty work, destroying the rainforests and the lives of those who inhabit them.

The Conquest of Papua

In his standard work from 2004 entitled 'World Agriculture and the Environment – A Commodity-by-Commodity Guide to Impacts and Practices', WWF visionary

Dr. Jason Clay claimed that in Indonesia alone there were still 20 million hectares of *"degraded"* land, which could be used for plantations. This number, which was presumably a relatively loose estimate, quickly found its way to the World Bank. It based its study 'Key Sustainability Issues in the Palm Oil Sector' on Jason Clay's figures and, on that basis, endorsed an expansion of the Indonesian palm oil industry by precisely 20 million hectares of *"degraded"* forest area.

In case there was any ambiguity, the World Bank study kindly provided a definition of *"degraded"* forest:

"Degraded forests are those in which the structure, species composition, biomass and/or canopy cover are reduced from what is considered to be the original pristine forest cover of the area."[71]

According to that definition almost every forest on earth could be classified as degraded, and thus earmarked for clearance – no matter how many human beings, great apes, tigers and elephants lived there. It just so happens that Cheng Hai Teoh, General Secretary of the WWF-founded Round Table for Sustainable Palm Oil (RSPO), had authored the World Bank study. Before that he had held a senior post at WWF Malaysia. Everything comes full circle in the end.

Thus a network of self-appointed favored few is deciding the fate of nations, and even entire continents. Jason Clay's studies and statistical slight-of-hand are eagerly adopted by the agribusiness lobby, which spreads the word like a virus at industry seminars and congresses. And very often, before you can say *"voluntary resettlement"*, it all ends in social violence.

Where exactly are those 20 million hectares of *"unused and degraded"* forestland that Jason Clay claims to have located in Indonesia? The island nation's main islands of Sumatra and Borneo have almost no primeval forest left to be cleared. Even the point men for the palm oil industry and the Indonesian Ministry of Finance in Jakarta put the country's potential for new plantations at just 10 million hectares at most. How did Jason Clay arrive at his 20 million? Had he perhaps included the land of the Papua in his calculation?

For years, the island of New Guinea, with its Indonesian provinces Papua and West-Papua, has been the Achilles heel of the Republic of Indonesia. Here there is still natural terrain as yet untouched by the ravages of the plantation economy – fertile land that agribusiness has long set its sights on. The main problem for the corporations is: this land belongs to the native Papuan tribes. Whoever would try to conquer it risks no less than war.

After the end of Dutch colonial rule, Indonesia forcibly annexed Papua, the western part of the island of New Guinea, and has since been engaged in trying to suppress the separatist ambitions of its people and to force them to assimilate. To break the resistance of the native peoples, a large-scale resettlement program has seen hundreds of thousands of people from other ethnic groups and other Indonesian islands moved into the conflict region. The Papua are now a minority in their own ancestral homeland, but they haven't given up on it yet; their bastion is the rainforest.

The right of the tribes to exploit the forests is anchored in the Indonesian constitution – a result of international conflict-resolution intervention. Now, in a final push to absorb the Papua into the Indonesian nation, the central government is planning to take their forest rights away, on the grounds that the province must be developed economically. If the government gets its way, Papua Province will be transformed into a paradise for industrial agriculture: sugarcane, wood and oil palms. The World Bank is taking care of the financial backing of the project, and the WWF helps deal with related ecological and social *"issues"* as they arise.

In April 2007, high-level representatives of the WWF and the World Bank met in Bali with the governors of the Indonesian provinces of Aceh, Papua and West Papua. The participants were gathered at this round table to discuss the future of the Indonesian rainforests: which forests could be exploited for *"sustainable economic development"* and which should be preserved so that they could be used to earn money from the UN program for *"avoided emissions"*? The central government in Jakarta had set the target: in Papua alone, 10 million hectares of forest would be felled to make way for plantations. The government was also planning to enact legislation that would allow it to give the corporations a 95-year lease on the land. The law makes provisions for compensation payments to expelled *"ethnicities"*.

At the close of the consultations the WWF and the World Bank announced their *"success"*: instead of 10 million, a mere 9 million hectares of rainforest had been earmarked to become *"economic zones"* in Papua. One million hectares would be maintained as national parks. In fact, the WWF had only been able to negotiate the protection of 500,000 hectares; the other 500,000 hectares had already been a legally protected national park before negotiations began. The WWF has also played an active, expediting role in the practical application of the Bali decrees: the organization has cast itself in the role of cartographer, mapping out the land of the natives.

Ronny is the project manager of the WWF West Papua office, located in Merauke. On his office wall hung a map showing the future zoning of Papua: where were the tribal holy places that had to be protected? In which areas

Ronny, WWF Indonesia

did the Papua have documented land rights, and where would the plantations go? The mapping process is a double-edged sword: in some isolated cases it can secure indigenous land rights; on the other hand, it can also legitimize the land grab of the invaders. When my journalistic colleague Inge Altemeier interviewed Ronny soon after the Bali meeting she asked him why the WWF stooped to aiding and abetting the industrial powers in their advance. His reply: *"There was no chance of saving the forest, so we had to work together with the companies, so that at least a few high-value forest areas would be protected."*[72]

The WWF man did not falter at the next question either. Who actually owned the forest that he was helping to divvy up? *"The local communities. The land still belongs to the tribes."* Did they know of the plan to plant 9 million hectares with oil palms? At this question Ronny shook his head and corrected me: *"Here in Merauke Province it's only a million hectares. The tribes have to be informed, so that they know what's being planned. Otherwise they won't give up their land. That would lead to conflicts. Some of them are concerned: where will I live if I sell off all my land? They can't imagine working on a plantation themselves one day. On the other hand, some of them think: If I sell up for a billion rupiahs, I can live on the money for 50 years. They* **have** *gotten the message."*

The WWF really does mean well, but had they ever bothered to ask the *"savages"* if they wanted to live in the brave new WWF world? It appears not. Their land is simply being subdivided into an economic zone and a nature reserve zone. The native inhabitants can no longer move freely in either.

On their visits to Papua villages WWF representatives tell the villagers that *"new job opportunities"* and *"new sources of income"* awaited them in tourism. In reality, these empty phrases amount to no less than the death of Papua culture. With the loss of their forest home the tribes also lose all traditional means of self-sufficiency and profitable production. They end up either as live exhibits in the ethnographic museum of the tourism industry, in the urban slums, or as underpaid casual laborers on the plantations. In the operation to expel the indigenous Papua the WWF has played the part of the advance guard, providing ideological flank defense. This role is reminiscent of that of the Catholic priests 500 years ago who went into the primeval forests of South and Central America to familiarize the natives with the benefits of *"civilization"*, easing the way for the Spanish Conquista that followed.

Kasimirus's Last Stand

Our journey throughout the green empire of the WWF ended in the village of the Kanume in Wasur National Park, on the border with Papua New Guinea. The terrain was austere: dry forests alternated with swampland. The WWF was proud of the fact that it had secured a safe haven for the Kanume tribe in the National Park, where they were safe from the clutches of the palm oil industry. My journalistic colleague Inge Altemeier paid a visit to Kasimirus Sanggara, chief of the Kanume, to ask him personally what he thought of the dramatic changes taking place in his homeland. On arrival she observed that the village of 90 families was under the guard of 80 Indonesian army soldiers. The national park was a heavily militarized zone – because the Free Papua Movement, OPM, was fighting with bow and arrow against the Indonesian occupiers. In the Wasur area everything was under control, but every Papua knew how calm was being maintained in the country: many Papua had been incarcerated, tortured and killed; some had vanished without a trace.

Inge Altemeier's filmed interview shows Kasimirus Sanggara in all his native glory, looking like he's dressed up for the role of tribal elder in a Hollywood film: his face is decorated with war paint; great plumes of feathers on his naked, muscular arms signify his powerful standing. He was the man with a direct line of contact to the gods of the forests and the owner of the only bicycle in the village. Although soldiers were on hand to *"supervise"* the interview, the chief nevertheless expressed criticism of the park regiment: his tribe was no longer allowed to keep pigs, and hunting was officially prohibited in the core zone of the park – for Kasimirus Sanggara an intolerable encroachment on tribal rights. The WWF offered in defense: although the hunt was officially forbidden, the authorities did in fact *"tolerate"* it. Conflicts with the palm oil industry were also out of the question, because according to the WWF, the entire Kanume tribal area was located within the Wasur National Park. Chief Sanggara, on the other hand, revealed that every year in June, at the beginning of the dry period, he would set off with his men for a five-month hunting foray beyond the boundaries of the park. The provincial government had promised there would be no plantations in the immediate area of

Chief Kasimirus Sanggara

the park but Kasimirus had no faith in the promises of the authorities.

He had become acquainted with the WWF in its role as mediator between the tribes and the occupying power: *"WWF staff were here to draw maps"*, the chief remembered. They, too, had made him many promises: a new village, money, a school, and the prospect of earnings for the tribe from the sale of their eucalyptus oil. According to Chief Sanggara, most of the promises had not been fulfilled, and he thus took a dim view of the WWF, whose envoys had also kept silent about plans to introduce a hunting ban in the park.

Kasimirus Sanggara had attended meetings with the chiefs of other tribes, where, among other things, they had discussed a government initiative known as MIFEE: the Merauke Integrated Food and Energy Estate project, the aim of which is to *"develop"* Papua economically. The Ministry of Agriculture wants to clear up to 1.9 million hectares of forest in Merauke district just to make room for oil palms, rice and sugarcane. The first agribusiness giants have already staked their claims in West Papua – according to the research of Marianne Klute (Watch Indonesia) 500,000 hectares were approved for clearance in 2012. There has been a massive increase in illegal logging even within Wasur National Park, in the heart of Kasimirus Sanggara's chiefdom – a sure sign of the rapid advance of agribusiness. Despite all the signs that should have triggered a red alert, to see that his world was facing certain demise was a stretch of the imagination too far for the chief.

With a sweeping gesture he described a circle in the air: *"The soldiers have good weapons, but they wouldn't do anything to me; they respect me. If I wanted to I could cast a spell on them. The Gods and our ancestors live in the forest. The forest is the source of life. We protect it – no one can destroy it."*

Acknowledgements

Without the generous help of friends and experts I would have been unable to adequately negotiate all the material on which this book is based. My heartfelt thanks, therefore, goes to those who kindly offered their valuable advice, helped with the wording and engaged in useful critical discussions on the manuscript: Inge Altemeier, Nina Holland, Klaus Schenck, Guadalupe Rodríguez, Ullash Kumar, Nordin, Prof. Andrés Carrasco (RIP 2014), Heribert Blondiau, Heike Schumacher, Konrad Ege, Raymond Bonner, René Zwaap, Reto Sonderegger, Javiera Rulli, Tibet Sinha, Arno Schumann and Marianne Klute. Very special thanks as well to the German TV broadcaster WDR, which allowed me to use the recordings and research data from my film 'The Silence of the Pandas'. I would also like to compliment my editor Hannah Blut on her astute questioning and fastidious post-research work, which put the crowning touch on this book. Last but not least, a big thank you to Ellen Wagner who worked wholeheartedly to create the precise and elegant English translation.

Wilfried Huismann

Born in 1951, Huismann studied history and social sciences. After a period as a development aid worker in Chile, he began his journalistic career in 1982 compiling investigative radio reports and authoring non-fiction books. Huismann went on to broaden his investigative scope to filmmaking, becoming one of Germany's most respected and successful documentary filmmakers. In recent years he has added screenwriting to his activities, including scripting episodes of the German cult crime series 'Tatort'. Huismann has been honored for his documentaries with three prestigious Grimme Awards in Germany as well as numerous international awards, including the World Medal at the New York Film Festival / BANFF Rockie Award / Certificato di merito silver, Prix Leonardo, Parma / Screening at Telluride Film Festival. Wilfried Huismann lives in Bremen, northern Germany.

Endnotes

All URLs were last checked on September 15, 2014.

1. Dowie, Mark, Conservation Refugees, Massachusetts, 2009, p. 123 et al.
2. Quoted from Dowie, op. cit., p. 130.
3. *Tiger in Not*, WWF Germany, Berlin 2010.
4. Quoted from Schwarzenbach, Alexis: *Saving the World's Wildlife. WWF - the first 50 years.* London 2011, p. 164.
5. Quoted from Bonner, Raymond: *At the hand of man. Peril and hope of Africa's wildlife*, New York 1993, p. 176.
6. Quoted from Bonner, op. cit., p. 176.
7. Bonner, op. cit., p. 178.
8. Quoted from Dowie, op. cit., p. 3.
9. Quoted from Douglas, Allen: *WWF. Rassenlehre und Weltregierung*, in: *Der Untergang des Hauses Windsor*, Wiesbaden 1995 (Publisher: Executive Intelligence Review), p. 21.
10. Quoted from Bonner, op. cit., p. 61.
11. Quoted from Bonner, op. cit., p. 64.
12. Interview with Kevin Dowling, 1997.
13. Quoted from Schwarzenbach, op. cit., p. 52.
14. Howarth, Stephen and Jonker, Joost, *A History of Royal Dutch Shell*, Band II, Oxford 2007, p. 427 et al.
15. Schwarzenbach, op. cit., p. 147.
16. Minutes from WWF executive committee from March 24, 1982, quoted from Schwarzenbach, p. 149.
17. Minutes from the WWF foundation council from April 26, 1967, quoted by Schwarzenbach, p. 148.
18. Kevin Dowling, unpublished Interview by René Zwaap, 1997.
19. Bonner, *At the Hand of Man. Peril and Hope for Africa's Wildlife*, New York 1993, p. 180 et al.
20. Bonner, op. cit., p. 77.
21. Quoted from Schwarzenbach, p. 219.
22. Interview with Kevin Dowling, 1997.
23. Quoted from Bonner, op. cit., p. 80.
24. According to Prof. Stephen Ellis, Leiden University, in a television interview with the author, March 7, 2011.
25. Schwarzenbach, op. cit., p. 218.
26. Groh, Dr. Arnold: *Report, Assessment and Recommendations regarding the Batwa people*, Press Office of the Berlin Technical University July 15, 2011.
27. *Locals who once opposed gorilla habitat now exert themselves to protect it*, Website WWF International from January 1, 2012
    URL: http://wwf.panda.org/what_we_do/how_we_work/conservation/species_programme/species_people/our_solutions/binp_uganda/

28. Ibid.
29. *Feasibility study Kavango-Zambezi-Project, Volume 2*
    URL: http://www.kavangozambezi.org/sites/default/files/Publications%20
    %26%20Protocols%20/kaza_tfca_prefeasibility_study_volume%202.pdf
30. MacDonald, Christine: *Green, Inc. – An environmental insider reveals how a good cause has gone bad*, Guilford 2008, p. 7.
31. Inge Altemeier conducted the interview with Amalia Prameswari.
32. Malaysian Environmental Consultants Sdn. Bhd., HCV Assessment of the Wilmar Central Kalimantan Project, Jakarta 2009.
33. Ibid. p. 16.
34. Wilmar, Central Kalimantan Project Indonesia – Proposed Conservation Area (owned by author).
35. Martina Fleckenstein in an interview with Inge Altemeier, 2010.
36. Greenomics, *Wilmar Touts Concern for Orangutan*, Jakarta, July 11, 2011.
37. Fleckenstein, Martina: *Roundtable on Sustainable Palm Oil*, presentation, GTZ, 2010.
38. Fleckenstein, Martina: *Umweltverbände schießen sich auf Nachhaltigkeitssiegel ein*, in: *top agrar online*, February 3, 2010.
39. http://www.iscc-system.org
40. *Cargill's Problems With Palm Oil*, www.ran.org/cargillreport
41. Sarawak Report: *Top US Economist Jeffrey Sachs was "cultivated" and "influenced" to become a "Champion" of Sime Darby*, November 2011.
    URL: http://www.sarawakreport.org/2011/11/top-us-economist-was-cultivated-and-influenced-to-become-a-champion-of-sime-darby-world-exclusive/
42. Sime Darby Website: Sustainability Initiatives, December 29, 2011.
    URL: https://web.archive.org/web/20120204013030/http://www.simedarbyplantation.com/Sustainability_Initiatives.aspx
43. Sarawak Report: *Top US Economist Jeffrey Sachs was "cultivated" and "influenced" to become a "Champion" of Sime Darby*, November 2011.
    URL: http://www.sarawakreport.org/2011/11/top-us-economist-was-cultivated-and-influenced-to-become-a-champion-of-sime-darby-world-exclusive/
44. The Telegraph: Palm oil round table "a farce", November 2008.
    URL: http://www.telegraph.co.uk/earth/environment/forests/3534204/Palm-oil-round-table-a-farce.html
45. WWF Deutschland, *Die »Heart of Borneo«-Initiative*, Frankfurt 2005, p. 2: www.wwf.de/downloads/publikationsdatenbank/ddd/10181/
46. Global Witness: *Pandering to the Loggers. Why WWF's Global Forest and Trade Network isn't working*, p. 8.
    URL: http://www.globalwitness.org/sites/default/files/library/Pandering_to_the_loggers_WEB.pdf
47. Clay, Jason W.: *Agriculture from 2000 to 2050 – The Business as Usual Scenario*, Global Harvest Initiative, speech manuscript, p. 36.
48. The Argentine foundation *Fundación Vida Silvestre* (FVS) joined the WWF International in 1988 and has been a member ever since.
49. Atlas del Gran Chaco Americano, GTZ 2006, p. 72.
50. Acta No. 4: *Foro por 100 Millones Sustentables*, September 14, 2004.

51. WWF press release from May 29, 2009: *Soy industry adopts environmental standards.*
    URL: https://web.archive.org/web/20090609151155/http://www.worldwildlife.org/who/media/press/2009/WWFPresitem12532.html
52. Blanco-Canqui, H., Lal, R.: *No tillage and soil-profile carbon sequestration: An on-farm assessment.* Soil Science Society of America Journal 72, 2008, p.s 693-701.
53. Altieri, Miguel, Bravo, E.: *The ecological and social tragedy of crop-based biofuel production in the Americas,* 2007
    URL: http://wrm.org.uy/oldsite/subjects/agrofuels/crop_based_biofuel.html
54. Roberts, Martin: *Limited biofuel land compatible with food*: www.Reuters.com (Spain) on May 19, 2010.
55. *Hungrig oder hurtig,* Süddeutsche Zeitung from December 12, 2013.
56. WWF Deutschland: *Searching for Sustainability,* November 2013
    URL: http://assets.panda.org/downloads/wwf_searching_for_sustainability_2013.pdf
57. RTRS_STD_001_V1-0_ENG_for responsible soy production: http://www.responsiblesoy.org.
58. The letter is from February 9, 2011 and was signed by Prof. Dr. Hartmut Vogtmann, Vice-president of the German Naturschutzring (DNR). The author owns a copy.
59. Clay, Jason: Speech at the Global Harvest Initiative conference, April 2010, Washington
    URL: http://vimeo.com/10776368
60. Ibid.
61. Clay, Jason: *How big brands can save biodiversity,* speech at the TED Global Conference, Edinburgh 2010
    URL: http://www.ted.com/talks/jason_clay_how_big_brands_can_save_biodiversity
62. *Blackwater's Black Ops,* The Nation, September 15, 2010
63. Hans Peter Fricker, head of WWF Switzerland, admits donations to Monsanto in an interview with the *Neue Zürcher Zeitung* from June 29, 2011: *Niemand beim WWF will ein Feigenblatt sein.*
64. *Note on the agreed WWF Network response to criticisms of WWF involvement in the Roundtable on Responsible Soy (RTRS) due to its links to Genetically Modified (GM) soy production.* WWF Internal Document from February 17, 2009. Sebastian Lasse gave it to the author.
65. Quoted from Winstra, Els and Rulli, Javiera: *El negocio de la Soja.* EcoPortal.net from October 10, 2005
    URL: http://www.ecoportal.net/layout/set/suscripcion/content/view/full/52665
66. Clay, Jason W.: *Indigenous Peoples and Tropical Forests. Models of Land Use and Management from Latin America.* Cambridge, MA: Cultural Survival, 1988. Cultural Survival Report 27.
67. Glasser, Jeff: *Dark Cloud: Ben & Jerry's Inaccurate in Rainforest Nut Pitch.* Boston Globe from July 30, 1995.
68. International Hydropower Association: *Hydropower Sustainability Assessment Protocol,* Sutton 2010

URL: http://www.hydrosustainability.org/IHAHydro4Life/media/PDFs/Protocol/hydropower-sustainability-assessment-protocol_web.pdf
69. The author has a copy of the letter from Minister Guy Lutgen dated September 9, 1997.
70. The author has a copy of the letter from James D. Wolfensohn (president of the World Bank) dated December 4, 1997.
71. Teoh, Cheng Hai: *Key Sustainability Issues in the Palm Oil Sector.* http://siteresources.worldbank.org/INTINDONESIA/Resources/226271-1170911056314/Discussion.Paper_palmoil.pdf
72. Inge Altemeier conducted the television interview with Ronny.

Picture Credits

p. 14 © Wilfried Huismann
p. 22 © Photo by Wilfried Huismann
p. 29 © WDR
p. 33 © Wilfried Huismann
p. 35 © Wilfried Huismann
p. 39 © Wilfried Huismann
p. 52 © Photo by Wilfried Huismann
p. 54 © Wilfried Huismann
p. 57 © Wilfried Huismann
p. 61 © Jan Schmiedt
p. 64 © Anonymous
p. 71 © Wilfried Huismann
p. 75 © Arno Schumann
p. 82 © Photo by Wilfried Huismann
p. 101 © René Zwaap
p. 115 © Arnold Groh
p. 120 © Photo by Wilfried Huismann
p. 123 © Wilfried Huismann
p. 126 © Wilfried Huismann
p. 133 © Wilfried Huismann
p. 134 © Photo by Wilfried Huismann
p. 146 © Inge Altemeier
p. 149 © Cordula Kropke / Rettet den Regenwald e.V.
p. 154 © Inge Altemeier
p. 171 © Photo by Wilfried Huismann
p. 172 © Photo by Wilfried Huismann
p. 179 © Wilfried Huismann
p. 180 © Marie Schumacher
p. 185 © Wilfried Huismann
p. 199 © Anonymous
p. 204 © Wilfried Huismann
p. 214 © WDR, Stefan Falke
p. 223 © Wilfried Huismann
p. 238 © Photo by Wilfried Huismann
p. 243 © Inge Altemeier
p. 247 © Inge Altemeier
p. 251 © Jan Schmiedt

Printed in Great Britain
by Amazon